What'd You Do
In The War,
Dad?

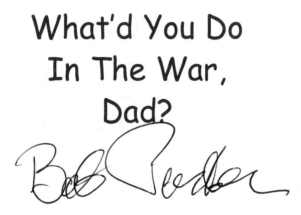

The author on skis, above Camp Hale, Colorado, 1944

What'd You Do In The War, Dad?

A Personal Look At 34 Months In The 10th Mountain Division

by
Robert W. Parker
Company E and Headquarters Company
87th Mountain Infantry

Rio Grande Publishing
Santa Fe

Published by: Rio Grande Publishing
                       304 Calle Oso
                       Santa Fe, NM 87501

Publisher's Cataloging-in-Publication Data
Parker, Robert W.
What'd You Do in the War, Dad?/Robert W. Parker. - 1st ed.
187 p.
Includes maps and photographs
1. World War II
2. Military
3. Combat
4. Italian Campaign

Library of Congress Control Number: 2005902367
ISBN: 0-9642561-0-X

**Cover photo: The author photographed his E-Company
comrades in 1943, climbing toward the summit of 13,200-
foot Homestake Peak, near Camp Hale, Colorado.**

DEDICATION

The memories recorded here are dedicated to the men of the 10th Mountain Division, killed or wounded on Kiska, or in the battles in the Italian Apennines and Alps. We whose lives or bodies were spared owe our remembrance of these stories to those heroic soldiers whose luck ran out on the battlefields of World War II.

TABLE OF CONTENTS

ACKNOWLEDGEMENTS

These stories could never have been recorded without the help of a number of friends and associates, whose memories and files are far better than my own. Many hazy details were clarified by Mary Hayes, Nat Holzer, Norma Johnson, Dee Molenaar, Harry Poschman, Sammy Sampson, George Senner, Dick Wilson and Dick Wright. Three marvelous pieces of art came from the artists, Captain George Earle of the 87th, Sergeant Armand Cassini of the 86th, and Sergeant Bob Fels of the 85th.

Photo illustrations, some of which I had never previously seen, were generously provided by Brad Boynton, Kathe Dillman, Dick Durrrance II, Newc Eldredge, Debbie Gemar of the 10th Mountain Resource Center, Jeff Leich for the New England Ski Museum, Phil Lunday, Dee Molenaar, Dick Rocker and Dick Wright.

Finally, I should recognize my daughter Katherine, her husband Mark Mikow, my son Guy, his wife Lori Cooke and their daughters Chandler and Arden. It was, after all, for them that this book was written.

INTRODUCTION

In 1941, I was a sophomore-level college dropout. I had sensed war was coming to the U.S., so I quit St. Lawrence College, learned to be a tree surgeon, and that December was working in Boston, trimming power lines and storm-damaged trees, when the Japanese attack on Pearl Harbor changed all of our lives.

Everyone in my hard working crew began to wonder how he could contribute to the war effort. On weekends, I haunted the Boston Harbor docks, thinking I might become a merchant mariner. But to join the cheapest maritime union, the electricians, cost sixty dollars, far more than an apprentice tree surgeon like me could afford.

I continued with my cold, dangerous, and dirty work, staying in a cheap boarding house, spending evenings in a nearby Christian Science reading room because it was a lot warmer than my unheated bedroom. One night, a few weeks after Pearl Harbor, I found an insignificant little two-inch story in the Christian Science Monitor that turned my life upside down.

It announced the formation of the 87th Mountain Infantry Regiment at Fort Lewis, Washington. The 87th was to be the U.S. Army's first winter warfare unit, to be trained for fighting in the mountains somewhere in this now global war. Unbelievably, the story said candidates for the 87th should contact the National Ski Patrol, and submit three letters of recommendation! The letters were to demonstrate the candidate's qualifications as a skier, mountain climber or experienced outdoorsman. I submitted three letters, one from my ski coach Otto Schniebs, one from my running and track coach, and one from an older friend, a skier.

Accepted, I joined the 87th, later to become the first of three infantry regiments in the 10th Mountain Division, in June, 1942. The stories that follow will attempt to answer the question posed by the title of this book: "What'd You Do in the War, Dad?" Most of these stories are not about the grim, dangerous and frequently fatal aspects of combat. They are about the sometimes humorous, frequently exciting, often heroic, occasionally bizarre behavior of men and animals training for and then experiencing the realities of war. Without exception, they were witnessed by or experienced by the author, who has only added certain dialogue and details to flesh out each story's reality.

Bob Parker
Santa Fe, NM

Mount Rainier, 14,410 ft. high. Muir snowfield is at the middle right, and Anvil Rock is the rocky point at the far right.

My Army Life Begins

Basic training at Fort Lewis, Washington, proved to be mostly standard infantry stuff; marksmanship, tactics, night bivouacs, and physical training. There were mountain-related differences; we climbed on an artificial climbing wall, some guys rode in a horse-mounted recon unit, and all of us had to attend our first mule-pack school.

But the weekends were another story. On our free time, we climbed in the nearby Cascade mountains, or journeyed to Mount Rainier for ice climbing and summer skiing. Weekends were the real beginning of our mountain training - here's how it was on Mount Rainier.

A DAY ON MOUNT RAINIER

It was the summer of 1942. We soldiers of the 87th Mountain Infantry Regiment, stationed at Fort Lewis, WA, spent many of our weekend days fishing on Puget Sound, or climbing in the Cascade Range, or exploring the almost pristine forested shores of the Sound. But our favorite destination, if we could get there, was Paradise Inn, at 5,400 feet on the flanks of snow-and-ice-covered Mount Rainier.

If we could get there! There were no regular buses. Few civilians had gas ration cards, or, for that matter, cars that were not up on blocks in the garage for the duration. There was no military traffic to Mount Rainier. So our only transportation was via hitch-hiking, sometimes on overloaded supply trucks for the Inn, with the rare Park Service rangers headed that way, and, occasionally (wonder of wonders!), with a civilian family, visiting the Park, or their daughters, working as waitresses or desk clerks, at Paradise Inn.

Mount Rainier was the closest training ground from Fort Lewis for mountaineering and skiing techniques. It offered the pristine snowfields, challenging rock faces, and towering seracs of blue glacier ice that we needed to hone our ice and snow and rock climbing skills. On one of our weekend expeditions, the challenge of Mount Rainier was to prove almost more than we could handle.

Some of our comrades, of course, preferred trips to Tacoma, or Olympia, or Seattle, all served by regular bus service, where legions of man-hungry young women were rumored to be waiting for virile mountain soldiers. But many of us, in love with mountains, and the techniques to conquer them, preferred our rugged but intensely satisfying expeditions on rock and snow. An early problem regarding access to Rainier was our heavy and cumbersome mountain gear. On our first forays, we carried packs, ropes, skis and poles, a sleeping bag and bulky mountain clothing. This at first represented a major inconvenience for hitch-hiking. But we soon learned we could cache our gear with the rangers, or with the wonderful young women who worked as waitresses or bartenders or cashiers at the Inn, or Paradise Lodge. Thereafter, we could confidently hitch hike in our dapper Class-A uniforms, change to climbing or skiing gear at the Lodge, and be on the mountain a half-hour after arriving at Paradise.

And What a Mountain

And what a mountain it was, especially to us Easterners or Mid-Westerners! At 14,410 feet, it ranked as one of the five highest mountains in the States. Rising almost literally from sea level, it was actually a bigger mountain than those in Colorado and California it was compared to; the standard summit ascent from Paradise Inn required an altitude gain of 9,010 feet, almost two vertical miles. A few of the men of the 1st Battalion of the 87th had climbed Rainier the previous spring, but all we had time for on our weekend adventures was to tackle the ice, snow, and rock below the 10,000 foot level.

Summer on Mount Rainier, however, was more than ice, snow and rock. Paradise Valley gained its name back in the 19th century for the glorious array of mountain flowers which sprang up in the surrounding meadows the minute the snows melted. The kaleidoscopic display of flowers, grasses and heather transformed the dull grass slopes left by melting snow and impressed even our European friends, who were used to the beauty of mountain flowers in the Alps. When our days on the mountain were over, we'd find a secluded waterfall or lake, strip off our clothes, cleanse our sweaty bodies

Summer on Mt. Rainier - weekend mountain recreation

in the shockingly cold water, rest briefly among the brilliant gentians and paintbrush and flowering heather to dry off, then dress and conduct a swift raid on the Inn's soda fountain. After a milkshake, or a sundae or banana split, it was time to set up a simple camp in a nearby grove of firs, where we troopers could spend the night less comfortably, but much more cheaply than in the very basic rooms available at Paradise Lodge for $5.00 a night for two persons

On this one most memorable weekend, five of us managed to hitch a ride on Friday afternoon on a supply truck that climbed all the way up the narrow, twisting highway to Paradise Inn. Here we splurged on a hamburger and milkshake for a 50-cent supper, collected our mountain gear, and retired to our fir-grove camp. We were four Easterners, Hawley, Len, Otto and myself, and Nap (short for Napoleon), from nearby Oregon. Before dawn, we had swallowed some hot tea and a K-ration, fastened mohair climbing skins on our skis, and after a brief hike through the sleeping meadows, fitted boots to bindings and started climbing the still frozen snow fields of Edith Creek Basin. This day, we had left our ropes, crampons and ice axes at Paradise, because we had planned several hours of skiing and picture taking on Muir Snowfield.

Climb to Camp Muir
The landmarks of our climb to Camp Muir, at 10,000 feet, are as clear today as they were almost 60 years ago. A gentle traverse up through Edith Creek Basin to a ridge from which we could look down into the shadows of the Nisqually Glacier canyon. Then, removing and shouldering skis, kicking steps up the face of Panorama Point, then, still on foot on frozen corn snow, climbing to a welcome break at McLure's Rock. At this point, we had ascended almost 2,000 feet and were ready to munch on a fruit bar, or suck on an orange scrounged from the mess sergeant back at the Fort.

At McLure's, we finally climbed into sunlight, having been in the shadow of Panorama Ridge until then. Above, the tumbled seracs of the Nisqually glowed blue-green in the early sun. To the west, the mountain's huge shadow still darkened the glacier canyons towards the ocean. Looking northwest, the distant snowy peaks of the Olympics were just catching the dawn sunlight. This kind of view was why the four of us from the East were in the mountain troops This was why we labored up the snowfields with heavy skis, instead of taking a bus to the civilized pleasures of Seattle.

Unbroken Whiteness
Above McLure's stretched the unbroken whiteness of lower Muir Snowfield, down which we intended to carve exhilarating tracks on our way off the mountain. But now it was a matter of pausing to spread zinc oxide on noses and lips, filling our lungs with the crystalline air of 7,000 feet above the distant ocean, then climbing, one ski ahead of another. Though we all hailed from sea

level homes, I don't recall that anyone had difficulty with the progressively rarified air. We were, after all, supposed to be physically fit mountain troopers.

As we climbed we began to make out the next landmark above us, the sharp, rocky tooth of Anvil Rock, with its tiny fire-lookout house. Here we hoped to find a summer ranger who could tell us where the best skiing might be found. Sure enough, as we slogged up the last slopes to the lookout, a figure appeared on the porch above us, and in a high-pitched Northwestern voice invited us in for coffee.

The summer ranger's name was George, from Seattle, and he was dying for company. For two weeks in a row, he lived alone in his crackerbox lookout, watching for the telltale smoke of a forest fire. Zeroing in on the fire with his glass-covered map and brass pointer, he would call in its location by radio. That was the only human contact he could expect from one end of the week to the other, and he was really glad to see us For half an hour we chatted and sipped on his day-old coffee, while he described his life as a fire lookout. His cabin was anchored to the rock with iron spikes and steel cable, and, we noticed, bristled with a porcupine-quill network of lightning rods.

"Anvil Rock is like a lightning rod, itself," he told us. "Thunderstorms break and this place lights up like Fourth of July. All you can do is climb into bed, and try to read a book while the lightning crackles and the thunder roars around you. Then after the storm, somewhere out there, a lightning-sparked fire will start, and my real job, spotting fires, gets under way again."

We wanted to hear more about life in this mountain aerie, but if we were going to ski we had to move on. Thanking George for his hospitality, we headed up on our skin-equipped skis for the final 500-foot climb to our destination, Camp Muir. Named for the famed naturalist John Muir, the camp proved to be nothing more than two squalid rock shelters, very much the worse for the incredible storms of wind, rain, ice and snow they had to endure on their exposed rock saddle between the snowfield and Cowlitz Glacier.

Skiing The Cowlitz

It was time to take the climbing skins off our skis, have a lunch break, and decide where to ski. George had advised against the Cowlitz side. The big crevasses were beginning to open underneath the covering snow. " Ski on the Muir side," he'd told us. It's a lot safer " But Hawley, Nap and Len were tempted by the apparently flawless slopes of the Cowlitz, stretching away endlessly below Muir Saddle. Against his better judgement, Otto joined them, and with a hiss of skis, the four disappeared onto the slopes of the Cowlitz.

Since I was not yet sure of myself on skis on steep, glacier slopes, I was content to practice quick slalom turns on the gentler corn snow of the Muir snowfield. So I would take eight or ten turns, climb back, and try to make ten tighter turns the next time down. I was totally engrossed in my practice when I heard a labored shout, and saw Otto leaning against one of the cabins, clearly out of breath. Scrambling back towards the saddle, I shouted, "What's wrong?"

Hawley's fallen into a crevasse," Otto gasped. "He's stuck on a ledge, so he's not hurt, but we've no rope, and no hope of getting him out." Then both Otto and I remembered - there had been a rope and ice axe on the wall in George's cabin. "I'm still fresh," I said, "I'll ski down to Anvil and get a rope and axe - maybe George will help." Grabbing my pack, parka and hat, and with no further thought, I launched myself into the 500-foot descent to the lookout. In spite of the emergency, it proved to be one of the most exhilarating ski runs I had ever had.

George acted almost as if he had expected me. With typical mountain-man sang-froid, he emptied a pot of hot tea into his thermos, tossed the tea, extra gloves and a sweater into his pack, gave me an extra parka to carry, and took down his axe and rope. After George radioed in that he'd be absent for a while, we set off on foot, me carrying my skis. In record time, we were at Camp Muir, then without skis, but roped together, we started down the long snow slope of the Cowlitz towards the group of tiny figures we could see far below. I prayed we would be in time.

Mount Rainier in summer with Nisqually Glacier center.
Cowlitz Glacier looms behind the two small pyramids, center right.

In One Piece

Our arrival at the crevasse, thankfully, proved anti-climactic. There on the snow sat Hawley, drawn and gray of face but clearly in one piece. Still snaking around and under him was the means of his salvation, a rope of tied-together climbing skins. (Otto told me later it had been his inspiration, at the Muir cabin, to collect our five pairs of skins, on the off chance they would be long and strong enough to effect a rescue.) Stuck deep in the snow were the skis and poles the group had used to anchor themselves. Exhausted from the effort and mental strain of hauling him out, the others sat numbly, catching their collective breaths.

I edged over to look down into the crevasse where Hawley had fallen. Beyond the tiny ice ledge where he had landed, all I could see were the apparently bottomless green-blue depths that would have meant certain death for our friend.

George and I roped Hawley in between us and returned slowly back to Muir Saddle. The others trailed behind, carrying their own and Hawley's skis, which they had first salvaged from the glacier with the help of George's rope. At the cabin, we warmed our victim with tea, got him to chew a candy bar, and began the nearly 5,000-foot descent to Paradise Inn. At the fire lookout, we returned George's gear, and thanked him warmly. In just a few hours, he had become, it seemed, like one of our oldest mountain comrades.

To The Edge of The Snow
    Instead of the glorious, swooping downhill we had envisaged, our progress toward the valley was now a series of slow snowplow turns, each of us carefully keeping Hawley at the center of the group. As dark fell on the snowfields, we relieved Hawley of his poles and pack, and Nap, supporting Hawley with a pair of climbing skin reins, and snowplowing carefully behind him, delivered him on skis the final 1,000 feet to the edge of the snow.

    Pooling our resources, we enjoyed a Spartan dinner at the Inn dining room. The Lodge management volunteered a room for Hawley, though the rest of us wearily trudged up to our sleeping bags in the trees. The next morning, a somewhat chastened group of mountain troopers said goodby to our kind hosts and rode another supply truck back to Tacoma, then a bus to Fort Lewis. It had been a day to remember, but not quite the day on Mount Rainier that we had dreamed of, just 48 hours before.

Postscript:

Six months later, I was walking toward the Service Club at Camp Hale, high in the Rockies of Colorado, when a soldier hailed me. It was George, the summer ranger from Mount Rainier. Inspired by the men he'd met from the 87th that summer, he had volunteered, and was now a fledgling member of the 85th Regiment, of the soon-to-be designated 10th Mountain Division.

San Antonio Mission at Jolon since restoration.
The original buildings dated from the 1700's.

California Coast Range Maneuvers

The war was not going well for the Allied Forces in the fall of 1942. The Japanese held much of southeastern Asia and the Pacific; Germany was still the master of Europe, North Africa and the Mediterranean. So our superiors in Washington, unsure what to do with us mountain troops, sent us to maneuver in the jungle-like California Coast Range, while our next training station, Camp Hale, in the more alpine mountains of Colorado was being constructed.

MANEUVERS, MULES AND MANZANITAS AT JOLON

As was usual in wartime, we, two battalions of the 87th, were traveling by train, with window shades rolled down, to an unknown destination somewhere south of Fort Lewis, Washington. As we rattled south, some of the most spectacular scenery in America unrolled around us, and we, for security reasons, could not enjoy it! All we could do was sleep, or play cards, or snack on the uninviting C-rations in our packs.

Our stay at Fort Lewis had been a combination of standard but strenuous basic training during the week, and varied, exciting, even exhilarating weekends. Now we were destined for some kind of maneuvers, probably in California, probably in the mountains, but none of us (except our close-mouthed officers) knew where!

As we wound southward that November, we had stolen glimpses of great rivers in Oregon, big redwoods in northern California, and teasing bits of civilization around San Francisco Bay. Now in the morning of the third day, some guys curious enough to lift our black-out curtains announced we were in flat farm country, with a hint of mountains to the west. And before long, with a tired screeching of brakes, and the hoot of our engine's whistle, we slowed and stopped.

A breath of hot, almost desert air swept into the stuffy atmosphere of the troop car as our doors were opened wide. Noncoms shouted orders, we straightened our uniforms, hoisted our barracks bags and descended into the California dust.

"Where the hell are we?" was on everyone's lips as we formed up in ragged platoon units and marched to a loading area swarming with trucks, jeeps and harassed looking officers. All around was the strong smell of livestock. Pens, corrals and barns confirmed this was cattle country. Several hundred yards away we could see a cluster of homes and small commercial buildings.

The announcement by one of our sergeants that we were in "King City, California" meant nothing to anyone, until a lieutenant, a Californian, attempted to explain. Scratching a crude map in the dust, he said "Here's Salinas to the north. Here's Paso Robles to the south. Here's King City, roughly in the middle. As you can see, it's a cattle town. That's the Coast Range (waving vaguely west). Nobody I know's ever heard of it, but we're going to maneuver near a place called "Holon". That's all I can tell you 'til we get there!"

More puzzled than ever, we sat on our barracks bags and gazed around us at the dry and dusty little cattle and railroad settlement. After misty, mountainous and forested Washington, what a place this seemed to be to send a bunch of mountain troopers!

Jolon With A "J"

But we were Army, so when the sergeants hollered for us to "mount up", we climbed, with our barracks bags, into the six-by-six trucks lined up for us. Soon the convoy began to move, dust began to swirl into the open truck backs, and we began the long slow trip to our mysterious destination. One of our Hispanic sergeants explained that "Holon" was spelled with a "J", and that the country we were headed for was once the site of a "Mission San Antonio."

"That's all I know," he admitted. "But this place was probably settled by Spanish missionaries, long before you guys' ancestors came over from Europe!"

So we ate dust, shifted our aching bodies, smoked and stared out of the truck's open back at the other trucks that wound up the road behind us. At the Mission, a cluster of half-ruined adobe buildings, we paused, every truck's motor running, while our officers studied their maps. We had been climbing through grazing country, then Ponderosa pines mingled with brush oak. When we started again, suddenly the terrain changed to open parklands studded with big boulders and massive old live-oak trees. Though still gravel covered, our road was so little traveled there was almost no dust. And as we looped around the road's many hairpins, we caught glimpses of tree-covered mountains to the west. Maybe this place called "Holon" wasn't going to be so bad, after all!

Pyramidal tents beneath the live oak trees

The Nacimiento

Our destination proved to be a rolling plateau of live oaks, boulders and a drying-up river called the Nacimiento. Like magic, it seemed, assisted by our strenuous efforts, our camp sprang from the dry leaves and grass of the plateau; pyramidal tents for the troops and officers, a big rectangular mess tent, another for the medics, water bags, a field shower, and off by themselves, canvas-enclosed slit trenches for toilet facilities.

After our first hot meal in days, the officers gathered us in the mess tent under the bluish glare of gas lanterns. Our colonel, Jefferson B. Willis, gave us an outline of our duties here at Jolon.

"First, I hate to tell you this," he began, "but Washington hasn't decided what to do with us mountain troops!" There was more than a little grumbling among the men - the prevailing scuttlebutt had already told us this.

"Just to cover their bets, they've sent us here to California for what they call Jungle-Mountain training! We start tomorrow with familiarization hikes, then the day after, when the mules get here, there'll be a new kind of training - that's all I can say about it, now!"

The Peaks of the Coast Range
Then he turned to some maps stretched between frames. "Here we are at Jolon. Just to the west, the peaks of the Coast Range; Cone Peak and Junipero Serra are the highest summits. Beyond, though we may never see them, Highway One and the Pacific. Southwest of us, Hearst's San Simeon estate. Due south, Camp Roberts Military Reservation, but we won't see any of it while we're here. With the war on, you probably couldn't find a lonelier stretch of country in America than this remote valley!"

As we scattered to our bunks, the talk was all about the mysterious "new kind of training" the colonel had mentioned. What could be so different from the varied rock and ice and rope and horse and mule training at Fort Lewis?

It turned out that it was not one day but three before we were to find out. Meanwhile, the mule skinners and cowboys in charge of our animals began setting up camp east of us. These guys were, in the vernacular, really pissed off at us infantrymen. Instead of riding trucks, most of them, except for a few horsemen, had walked their mules all the way from King City! It was thick dust, and mule shit, and a long hot, hard slog from the hot plains to the foothills until finally they arrived on this relatively cool and shady plateau, to find us already ensconced in the choicest campsite!

Lethal Looking Machetes

But we didn't have time to respond to their epithets. On the first day, we broke up into company units, and walked an easy five miles into the hills, along old game and burro trails. On the second, it was a longer, circuitous route, at least ten miles into and out of steep canyons, up some steep, rocky hogbacks and then back along a forest road into camp. The third day, we were issued machetes, long, lethal-looking blades of steel, with leather sheaths to hold them on our packs.

Noting our curious glances and comments about the machetes, the captain called for silence. "They call these maneuvers "Jungle-Mountain" exercises." he noted. "Today you'll find out why! No more trails or roads. No more cool snow or rain. We will cut our own trails. Each man will lead a column, until everyone has practiced with a machete. Then, next week, you'll have a chance to test your new skills against a real enemy!"

And it was on this day we learned about the "manzanita", an enemy so obdurate that we all wondered what "real enemy" could be tougher!

For the mountainsides we now confronted were covered with a thick growth of a shrubby evergreen tree most of us Easterners had never encountered. With glossy green leaves, orange bark partly covered with a nearly black skin, the manzanita also boasted the toughest, hardest, sharpest branches nature could have invented! As we slashed and hacked and scrambled our way up these otherwise innocuous looking slopes, our machetes grew dull, our skin scratched and bloody, our shirts soaked with sweat and our minds finally realized the full impact of the phrase "jungle mountains."

As we took a break on a small bench, our platoon leader slumped beside us. "Makes the Alps look inviting," he said, grinning. "If our leaders in Washington could see us now, I know they'd find something for us to do in Europe!"

Years later, remembering that moment, some of us

wished "our leaders" had sent us to the mountains of New Guinea, instead of to the Italian Apennines. But our jungle training that day was just the beginning. We learned to carry whetstones, to keep our machetes sharp. We discovered which brush or tree or plant could be cut easily, and which, like the manzanita, had to be hacked out of the way. We even learned to coat ourselves with fly dope from the mule skinners, to keep the worst of the buzzing, biting insects at bay. And that weekend, we found out who the "real enemy" was that the captain had been talking about.

The Filipino Scouts

Some of us had read newspaper accounts of a mysterious special unit, made up of men who had escaped the Philippines, or were living in the States, called by the newspapers the Filipino Scouts. They were rumored to be tough, angry patriots, eager to return and fight the Japanese in their homeland.

On Saturday, soon after we had been marched in formation to our open field parade ground, a convoy of six-bys arrived at our motor pool. Out of each truck descended a squad of Aussie-style-hatted, khaki uniformed, brown skinned soldiers, until a battalion of them had formed up opposite us. Their officers saluted ours, and our colonel stepped forward.

"Gentlemen!" he began, which was startling enough in itself - usually it would have been "Men!" or "Soldiers!" "I want you to meet the first battalion of the U.S. Army's First Filipino Regiment!. For the next week, we'll be maneuvering against them here in the Coast Range. As of tomorrow, we won't know where they are camped, or where their positions are. We, and they, will be competing for the same objectives. In effect, we'll be enemies! Any questions?"

A ripple of laughter passed through our ranks, but no questions were forthcoming. The apparently expressionless faces of the Filipinos remained without expression.

"Very well," the colonel continued. "You'll get your orders at the platoon and company level tomorrow. Meanwhile, no weekend leave or time off until these maneuvers end!"

We and the Filipinos stood at attention in the hot California sun until the colonel had chatted with their officers. Then, without any obvious spoken orders, the brown-skinned battalion returned to their trucks, climbed in and whirled away as if they'd never been with us at all. Their sudden departure, we would learn, was typical of the illusive qualities of this new and clearly different force we were to maneuver against!

Well, to put it simply, these were the strangest maneuvers a U.S. Army unit had ever, until that time, found itself involved in. Not only were the Filipinos illusive, but if the truth be known, whatever the official record shows, they defeated us American mountain troops handily, in almost every exercise!

Everything On Their Backs

Above all, it was their mobility. While we moved through the twisted ridges and canyons of the Coast Range, with mules and horses carrying men and supplies, the First Filipino soldiers apparently carried everything, including food and water, on their backs. While we, with few exceptions, had to hack our way noisily through low trees and brush with our machetes, our enemy were small enough to slip beneath the heavy forest cover, arriving at their objectives almost as silently as ghosts.

To those who knew a little history, it was like the 18th century British soldiers versus the eastern Indian tribes. Except, of course, the British Army had nothing to deal with as cantankerous and stubborn as our Missouri mules.

When we were trying to be silent, our mules brayed or snorted. When we needed a particular pack-load of supplies, like as not the mule carrying it got stubborn and refused to move. One mule fell down a steep moun-

29

tainside carrying two weeks' supply of tomato ketchup. When his handler got down to him, and saw him lying silent, covered apparently with blood, he called for a .45 pistol to put the beast out of its misery.

That Bloody Mule
   While he was calling for a gun, the mule woke up, got to his feet, and started up the canyon on his own. The mule-skinner never heard the last of this event, known to his buddies as "George and that Bloody Mule!"
   The Jolon maneuvers will long be known for other nasty aspects of the Coast Range. Several guys settled their sleeping bags into comfortable-looking ivy thickets, only to wake up with serious poison-oak infections. There were broken legs, mule kicks and bites, one case of snake bite (we never saw the snake!), and many cases of blistered feet and raw, red sunburn. Myriad flies, mosquitos and other flying, crawling things affronted our already sensitive eastern, northern or middle-western skins.
   But there were a few highlights on our side. One of our lieutenants, perhaps remembering some of George Washington's early successes against the Indians, decided to out-think the Filipinos. Having noted they didn't seem to like maneuvering at night, he led a company of volunteers up a mountainside in the dark, crawling under, rather than hacking through the manzanitas.
   By midnight, his men lay just below a mountain summit. At dawn, they swarmed over the Filipino outpost guards, captured the summit, and radioed back their success. Our side got a victory, (eerily prefiguring our later success on Riva Ridge), the lieutenant a promotion, and the Filipinos perhaps their first realization that the American mountain troops might not be the pushovers they had initially thought.
   One special advantage our company had was a veteran private from somewhere in Montana whom we knew as Indian Joe (not his real Blackfoot name.) From

our first day at Jolon, Joe had obtained permission to add to our uninspiring larder by "requisitioning" some of the mule deer that roamed the hills around the camp. I remember him patiently filing the points off some of our copper-tipped target rounds, then filing grooves in the tips to make what we used to call "dum-dum" bullets.

Around sunset, he'd take his Springfield sniper's rifle and a pocket full of dum-dums into the forest. In a surprisingly short time, we'd hear a shot, then Joe would quietly reappear and ask for man or two to bring out his kill.

Venison Steaks

For several weeks, our company would feast on delicious venison steaks, roasts and "liver and lights" while the Filipinos were subsisting on the usual Army canned beef and beans.

Our six weeks in Jolon provided a jarring reality check for both the enlisted men and officers of the "elite" 87th mountain troopers. But when orders came in December to leave for our new training center in Colorado, most of us were proud of our newfound skills, our endurance, and our tested and toughened physical condition.

We never saw the men of the First Filipino Regiment again. But they had played a major role in preparing us for a difficult winter at Camp Hale, and the ordeals of Kiska Island later the next summer. For those who made it through "Jolon," our pre-combat activities would never seem as tough as the maneuvers, manzanitas and mules in the Coast Range of California.

Nick Paske and Dick Wright, with 13,200 foot
Homestake Peak in the background.

Into the Snow at Last

After the end of the Jolon maneuvers, we rode the train
from California to Camp Hale, arriving on Christmas Eve,
1942. Suddenly we were involved in an entirely different
environment. At 9,200 feet above sea level, Hale was as cold
and snowy and alpine as Jolon had been like the jungles of
Asia. We soon were issued winter clothing and gear, trained
on skis at Cooper Hill, our 11,000-foot-high ski slope facility, and frosted our feet and hands at Hale's snow-covered firing ranges.

In February, scarcely six weeks adjusted to our winter
surroundings, we were trucked up to Cooper Hill. After an
uncomfortable night in the crowded barracks at Cooper, we
fell out in the morning with full field packs and weapons. Our
destination on skis and snowshoes was a nearby 13,000 foot
mountain. It was the initial Homestake maneuver, the first
regimental-size high altitude winter maneuver ever attempted by the U.S. Army.

ARTILLERY VERSUS AVALANCHE ON HOMESTAKE PEAK

Though the roar of the four Pack 75's had subsided, echoes still rumbled around the sides of the cirque valley where we stood. Every soldier's eyes, whether general's or captain's or buck private's, were fixed on the long wall of snow cornice that hung above us. At first, not a foot of that shell-battered wall seemed to move. Then suddenly cracks splintered the snow, huge chunks began to crumble, and before our eyes tons of snow began to slide. Avalanche! Which was exactly why we men of the 87th Mountain Infantry, and attached units, were on the shores of Slide Lake that day.

For us mountaineers in training, it began on a sub-zero morning in February, 1943, at the old barracks at Cooper Hill, our ski-instruction slope. With 90 pounds or more in our rucksacks and on our backs, we set out on skis and snowshoes for a camp-site somewhere on 13,200-foot Homestake Peak. All we knew that morning was that we'd be living in the snow for more than a week, and had to carry everything we'd need, except for a few special rations.

Our route led down to Tennessee Creek at 10,100 feet, then climbed up an old wood road towards the camp site at 11,200 feet. Though we infantrymen thought our 90-pound loads were heavy, our machine gun and mortar men were carrying, with mortar base plates and barrels, or machine gun barrels and tripods, as much as 125 pounds.

Stopping where we crossed the old Highway 24, we skiers fixed mohair climbing skins on our skis, and started to climb. Those of us fresh from maneuvers in California's Coast Range knew right away we had a real advantage in physical conditioning. Many others, some of them just arrived from sea-level Army camps, were in for a tough day at two miles high.

At first, most men were fresh enough to keep up with the column. Given the circumstances, our officers called for 10-minute breaks every half hour. But soon men were failing to get up after a break. It became obvious, that it would be a bitter struggle for some to make it to the 11,200 feet bivouac site.

Our company commander, seeing the problem, told the better climbers to go on ahead, set their own pace, and set up camp at the designated site. So some of us went on ahead, and by mid-afternoon, we had arrived at a sign that said "E-Company Bivouac." As we were climbing, we had been talking about the guys we'd left behind. A few of us hurriedly put up mountain tents, while others emptied packs and gear into the tents. With empty packs on our backs, and a few men left behind to guard our gear, we headed down the trail on skis to see if we could help our more heavily laden comrades.

Rescue Mission

Our hasty rescue mission was badly needed. Many of the weapons platoon guys had just plain tuckered out, and lay by the trail, propped against their pack boards. Once we took over carrying their personal gear, most were revived enough to struggle on with their weapons. Others were hauled to timberline on weasels, our tracked over-snow vehicles. Ultimately, most of the regiment reached the bivouac site before dark. The maneuver judges, however, gave us all a day of rest, having learned hard lessons about the limits of heavily laden soldiers at high altitudes.

During the rest day, we had time to learn some tricks

of living in the snow from our Finnish and Norwegian old timers. One of these tricks was setting up our poorly designed "mountain tents" in neat rows, designed to please military-minded officers at inspection time. Then each pair of tent mates sought out nearby banks of snow or tree-sheltered hollows, carved out a snow cave, and slept in the cave for the rest of the maneuvers. Snow caves are much cozier than the frost-plagued, frigid tents we were supposed to sleep in.

Cook's Cavern
Our Finnish mess sergeant taught us another cold weather comfort solution. Instead of dozens of cooking fires, or cooking over our gasoline mountain stoves, he sent us out to collect piles of dead wood in the virgin spruce forest, to add fuel to a central fire. The huge blaze we created soon burned a deep, rounded cavity, right down to bare ground, in the eight or ten feet of accumulated snow. Inside this open-ceilinged cavern, we cooked on the fringes of the constant bonfire, ate, smoked and enjoyed a communal warmth vastly more comfortable than in the frosty confines of our tents.

Our Norwegian comrades taught us to rub bacon grease into our hands, and on noses and ears, to avoid frost bite. They demonstrated how two buddies could avoid frozen feet by sitting opposite one another, and holding one guy's stockinged feet against the other's warm belly. Though the bacon grease, and the smudge and smoke in our "cavern', ruined the pristine white of our winter uniforms, the tradeoff in comfort was such that our officers, by and large, overlooked our less than parade-ground appearances.

And we needed to know all we could about living in the snow in February, at above 11,000 feet. Headquarters radio picked up a weather report from the Eagle valley: 48 degrees below zero at 8 a.m. When I put on my steel-rimmed glasses to read the label on a food can that morning, the rims shattered in a dozen pieces. Picking the lenses out of the snow, I stuffed them in a pocket, where they remained for the rest of the maneuvers.

Before the rest day was over, assignments were given out by our platoon leaders. Our squad was lucky - a patrol with skis to the top of Homestake Peak! Others were to practice with our various weapons, or set up defensive positions in the snowy woods. But the big news, and hardest assignment, was to assist the artillery in placing four Pack 75's, so called because they could be disassembled to ride on pack mule's saddles, in position for a history-making effort. They would attempt to shoot down an avalanche from the snow-laden corniced eastern ridge of Homestake Peak!

But first, our squad would have a chance to climb the east ridge, then ski down the south ridge of the peak before the avalanche experiment began. This was nominally an armed reconnaissance, so some of us carried our Garand rifles and two clips of blank ammunition. Sergeant Birger Torrison might have had some live rounds in his pocket, just in case we ran into some of those wary but extremely edible ptarmigan out there in the snow.

After a quick breakfast in the cook's cavern, we set out on skis for the foot of the east ridge. As I recall, there were eight of us, Sergeant Torrison, Warner, Landry, Paske, Rocque, Korban, Wright and myself. It would be uphill all the way to the peak, so we affixed climbing skins immediately.

Wax Wizard

We rookies did, at least. But Torrison, a wizard with ski wax, had applied one of his secret mixes to his ski bottoms, and climbed easily, without skins, at the head of our little column.

At first it was just another Colorado mountain slope, dotted with spruce trees, and covered with dry powder snow. Then as we gained elevation, the slope became a rugged above-timberline ridge. We zig-zagged across it until its west face became a cliff, and we were forced, in single file, to follow Torrison's narrow track around onto the ridge's rocky eastern side. Just as some of us began to question our leader's steep and airy route, he stopped. "Ve'll carry our skis from here," he said. "Too steep, and ve might cut a slide!"

Shaking out our skins, and stowing them in our packs, we continued to climb, this time with skis on our shoulders, in the deeply kicked steps of our leader. For the first time at Camp Hale, I began to feel like a mountain trooper; skis, rifle and pack on my back, climbing an ever steeper slope with an armed enemy (if only imaginary) somewhere on the heights above us.

Soon Birger asked us, one at a time, to lead. My turn came as the slope seemed almost perpendicular. Immediately I felt that the whole party's safety now depended on how carefully I chose the route, and kicked each step. Luckily, it wasn't long before the face sloped back, the wind increased sharply, and we found ourselves on Homestake's broad eastern shoulder.

Leaning Into the Wind

Here the skis became a sudden danger, catching the wind like tall sails. Birger set the example, putting down his skis, and kneeling to fix boots into bindings. When all were ready, the Norwegian led the way along the ridge westward, each of us leaning into the wind, setting our edges sharply into the hardened snow crust of the cornice where it met the wind-scoured rock of the ridge. It seemed forever (see cover photo) before we reached the snow covered summit of the mountain, and turned to look back along our route, and down over the steep cirque walls into Slide Lake Basin.

Torrison couldn't resist a survival lesson. "See how I stayed vell away from the edge of the cornice?" he queried, almost shouting against the wind. "No way to know how far out ve could go before it vould break, and give us a ride down to the lake!"

Atop Olympus
Far below us, we could see four teams of men and clusters of officers, maneuvering the four 75 mm. cannon into position on the far side of the snow-covered lake. In a day or two, we were to witness the historic avalanche experiment. But meanwhile, we felt a little like gods atop Olympus, while some of our buddies wrestled with the weapons of Mars below.

All this while on the summit, the bitter wind was trying to pry under our wind-proof parkas, forcing us to think about hot coffee and warm sleeping bags. While we hurriedly rubbed downhill wax on our ski bottoms, Torrison stood there shuffling his skis in the fine powder.

"If you guys vould yust learn how to vox, you could be skiing, now," he grinned. "See how my vox is yust as good for downhill as for up!" With that, he gave a powerful shove on his poles, and set the first track down the south ridge.

Smooth Christies
One by one we followed, most snowplowing carefully, since this upper ridge fell away for hundreds of feet on either side. But Torrison, acting as if this were just a practice slope, was cutting smooth christies and singing to himself in Norwegian. How long would it be before we were as at home in the mountains as this Norske strong man?

Where the ridge broadened, and the snow softened, we too began to enjoy the descent. It seemed only minutes before we left the ridge, and continued linked turns down to the first timberline trees. Here Birger stopped, and waited for the last skier.

"Ve don't vant people to think this trip vas fun," he

laughed. "So let's ski into camp by the numbers, like a proper ski patrol!" Once out of the woods, after 'an exhilarating 2,000-foot descent, we formed a line behind Torrison, and slid up to our tent line "by the numbers."

"You're a good squad," the Norwegian said, as he shook each man's hand, "even though you don't know how to vox!" For me at least, this quiet comment was the highest kind of praise from a great skier and mountaineer like Birger Torrison!

The next day was a huge letdown, after the thrills of Homestake. As I remember, we maneuvered among the timberline trees, setting up lines of fire and defensive positions to the satisfaction of our officer referees. All of the talk that day was about the avalanche experiment, coming up on the morrow. During a break, one of the officers gave us a brief history of the terrible days during World War I, when thousands of Austrian and Italian soldiers, fighting in the Dolomite and Julian Alps, were killed in avalanches, many of them triggered by artillery shells, or detonated land mines.

"No one thinks we'll ever have to fight under those conditions," he continued. "But the generals want to know if our artillery can knock down slides. That's one of the main purposes of these maneuvers!"

Will the Cornice Come Down?

At supper that night, the men who had the artillery assignment filled us in. "They dragged the guns up to the lake with weasels, then we manhandled them into position," a sergeant said. "They'll fire one round per gun, then if it doesn't trigger a slide, four more rounds. Nobody knows whether, after all our work, that cornice will come down!"

Next morning, after the usual GI routines, we stacked our skis, stowed guns and gear in our tents, then marched in ski boots up to the lake. Assigned positions on the moraine ridge that formed the south shore, and across the lake from the corniced face, we stood impatiently, staring at the unaccustomed actions of the artillerymen, and stamping our feet to stay warm.

It must be said that someone on the maneuver staff had chosen the site well. Slide Lake sits in an amphitheater-shaped cirque, or glacier-cut gouge in the lee side of Homestake Peak. All along the mountain's east ridge, the winter's unusually deep snow had formed a wind-deposited cornice or drift, which we had climbed up two days before, but which now loomed over us, a wall of snow capping the 1,000-foot face of the cirque.

The Cannonade

Set well back at the edge of the woods, and with barrels tilted sharply up, the four 75 mm cannon, stood ready. When the requisite colonels, generals and visiting civilians had all arrived by weasel and taken their places in a rank in front of us, it was time for the cannonade.

A ski trooper examines a block of ice, thrust up from Slide Lake by the avalanche

We all flinched at the incredible echoing and re-echoing roar of the guns in that natural amphitheater. After the first four rounds, the blast of a second four assaulted our ears as we stared up at the four spouts of snow erupting across and just under the lip of the cornice. For a moment, nothing moved, and we remembered the sergeant's words "Nobody knows whether that cornice will come down!"

Then the cornice seemed almost to shiver, as cracks split its face, and chunks of snow as big as houses began to slide. First the pack artillery guys began to cheer, then the officers and guests, and finally we all were cheering as the mass of snow ponderously gained headway. When the avalanche hit the talus slope at the cirque's base, a blinding cloud of powdered snow arose, and rolled across the lake directly at us. Enveloped in its swirling fog, we at first didn't realize the second, unexpected outcome of the avalanche.

The Ice is Moving!

Our captain might have been the first to give a warning. "The ice!" he hollered."The ice is moving! Keep an eye on the lake!"

Our place on the moraine was safe enough, so we stared through the fog of snow at this new phenomenon. The officers and guests, however, in their preferred position on the shore in front of us, had to scramble desperately to get clear of this unexpected danger.

For, to everyone's surprise and amazement, the tremendous weight of the huge avalanche the Pack 75 shells had released was shoving the lake's six-or eight-foot ice covering out of the lake and up on the shore, directly at the dignitaries lined up to watch the avalanche!

Probably two-thirds of the lake's ice was deposited, in this impromptu fashion, on the sloping gravel shore. Once the cloud of snow, and sound of falling rocks and grinding ice had diminished, we all straggled down to gaze in astonishment at the results of the avalanche's power. A broken plaque of blue green ice, six or more feet thick and as wide as the lake was long, occupied the lake shore's former reviewing stand. The previously snow-mantled wall of the cirque now stood nearly bare of snow, the grim aspect of its rocky, vertical cliffs revealed.

41

I've often wondered if the official write-up of this, the one and only similar experiment, to my knowledge, ever conducted by the U.S. Army, even mentioned the scrambling embarrassment of the reviewing officers, as snow clouds and ice blocks forced them to retreat.

At any rate, the artillery versus avalanche question was rousingly validated. And those of us who witnessed the result were forever grateful that we would not have to test this historic killing method in combat, in the forbidding mountains of Hitler's "Festung Europa."

Sgt. Jim Fenton stands guard between Canadian
and American flags on Kiska, with task force craft in
the background in the frigid waters of the Bering Sea.

Part of the Aleutian War

My regiment, the 87th, had trained at Camp Hale only five months, and had begun to feel we were really mountain soldiers, when orders arrived to send us to Fort Ord, California for amphibious exercises! Not knowing even what "amphibious exercises" meant, we nonetheless packed up, traveled by train to Ford Ord, near Monterey, and frustrated, found ourselves repeating our Fort Lewis infantry basics.

Some of us were almost ready to transfer out of the 87th in sheer disappointment, when we were trucked one day to Monterey Bay, and were loaded aboard an old troop ship, where several tough and grizzled Marine sergeants began our amphibious training.

Daily, we were conveyed out to the troop ship by landing craft, climbed up landing nets with full field gear, then descended the landing nets into the landing craft until our mentors thought we were actually ready to do an amphibious landing. After three weeks of exercises along the California coast, when we actually rode the Higgins boats through the surf and waded ashore to engage an imaginary enemy, we loaded into larger troop ships in San Francisco harbor and set sail - northward!

It was here, as part of a combat-ready convoy, we finally learned our destination. It was the Aleutian Islands, and the Japanese-held island of Kiska!

OFFICER OVERBOARD!

It was our D-Day, August 15, 1943, on board a small Higgins landing craft heading straight for the northwest coast of Kiska Island, close to the western end of the Aleutians, and only two thousand miles from Japan. Some of Recon's thirty men were mingled with men from a line company, whose designation I should not reveal. As far as we knew at that moment, the men of the 87th Mountain Infantry were going to war.

Under the thunder and lightning of an intense naval bombardment of the island by the battleships of the North Pacific fleet, we had climbed that morning, in full battle gear, down the rope nets hanging from the gunwales of our troop ship into our landing craft. Spread out in line with us was an impressive array of craft like ours, escorted by destroyers, all headed for an anticipated fierce reception ashore by the Japanese enemy.

Huddled together in the rear of the LCVP, we had little thought for anyone or anything but the battle we believed awaited us on Kiska. The bombardment from naval guns, as well as the array of landing craft, destroyers, and battleships with us seemed evidence enough that a well armed, well fortified enemy lay in wait on the precipitous mountain slopes looming ahead of us.

It was with only mild interest at first, therefore, that we watched a line company master sergeant talk with the Navy boatswain who commanded the LCVP on the craft's bridge, then climb down to whisper to our lieutenant. Observing the lieutenant's already strained face

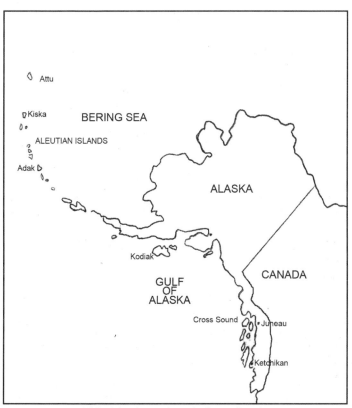

Kiska Island was closer to Japan than to
Seattle, Washington, 2600 miles to the southeast

turn pale, we suddenly knew that all was not well on our
wave-battered little metal and plywood vessel.

When the sergeant moved forward, the lieutenant
circled his hand over his head in the signal for us to
gather around him. A finger against his lips, he whispered hoarsely to those of us who could hear him.

"Something totally against orders is going to happen
up forward in the line company," he said. "I cannot - I
should not, have anything to do with it! Neither should
any of you, in my opinion!"

Then he was silent, and when our platoon sergeant
pressed him for more information, he shrugged. " You'll
see, you'll see!" was all he said. Then he turned, and
stared up at the boatswain at the wheel with a tense,

pained frown on his face.

Clearly disturbed, the sergeant whispered to us. "OK, guess that's it. For now, no questions, and we stay put where we are until we see what's going to happen!" For a while, there was nothing unusual going on except the waves pounding inches away on the outside of our thin Higgins boat shell, and the growling of the engine that propelled us. Then we could see a stirring among the line company soldiers crowded amidships.

A Terrified Shout

Suddenly, a terrified shout rose above the soldiers' voices. "No! You can't! God damn it, you can't!" A knot of men, gathered tightly around a man we could see was an officer, shoved him toward the steep wall of the LCVP, then bodily lifted him, and hurled him, screaming, over the side into the frigid waters of the Bering Sea.

None of us, jammed between the walls of the narrow boat, could see anything of the drama that must have been unfolding in the water. The boatswain, his Army counterpart and the machine-gunner stared back over their shoulders, but the craft maintained its bearing straight for the shores of Kiska. It was as if nothing had happened to interrupt our inevitable progress towards war.

On the LCVP, we heard nothing more, but that the men of that line company had decided they'd never go into combat with their hated captain, and to make sure, had hurled him overboard. A short while later, the stressful, dangerous events of our landing began, and all thought of the disgraced and possibly dead captain disappeared from our minds.

Except for the fortunate lack of enemy fire, it was not an easy landing. Many of the landing craft hung up on surf-hidden rocks, unable immediately to unload their cargoes of men and gear. Our craft dropped its ramp well out from shore, so we waded, rifles and machine guns held overhead, through chest high water to the rocky beach, and set up a hurried firing line behind the wave-cut bank at the foot of the mountains facing us.

To my knowledge, there were no casualties except

Landing craft headed for the Bering Sea invasion side of Kiska Island. Note the fog shrouding the mountain summits.

plenty of sea-water soakings among the men landing at our cove, a brief opening in the island's rocky north-western wall. Almost at once, never mind our wet clothes and equipment, the order came to start climbing the steep rock and grass covered slopes that rose in impressive folds out of the sea. Soon involved in the mountain's steepness, thoughts of the still invisible enemy, and the fog that curled everywhere around us, we not surprisingly forgot the life-and-death struggle we had witnessed on board our cockle-shell landing craft.

The Amazing Sequel

It was days later, after we discovered there were no Japanese left on the island, that we were able to piece together the amazing sequel to the "officer overboard" incident. To give those angry infantrymen credit where it was due, we learned they had done everything in their power to save their captain's life. They first stripped him of all his heavy gear - pack, pistol belt, pistol and helmet. They had released the CO2 capsule, inflating his life belt, and threw overboard with him an opened packet of the life-saving bright orange dye issued by the Navy. They also had asked the Navy bosun to radio "man-overboard" to the nearest destroyer, but his orders for "radio silence" made that impossible.

Nonetheless, our destroyer escort put on an incredible display of seamanship. Apparently viewing the incident through field glasses, its commander turned his destroyer almost on its stern, steered towards the bright orange dye, and ordered the unlimbering of a motor driven rescue dory. Literally within minutes, the rescue crew hauled the captain out of the 50-degree water, wrapped him in blankets and motored back to the destroyer, where Navy medics took over and revived him, little the worse physically for his experience.

The Captain's Future
We were equally impressed by the manner in which the task force commander, General Corlett, handled the captain's future. After questioning him carefully, the general kept him in confinement-to-quarters until a ship was available bound back to the States. In Seattle, he was interrogated again, stripped of his rank, and discharged, without prejudice, from the service.

The master sergeant involved later received a battlefield commission to Second Lieutenant, and served with distinction until the end of the war. As far as I know, none of us heard any further news of the officer who was thrown overboard on the day of our landing on Kiska. Years later, we heard many more stories of feared and hated officers who were variously shot, or "fragged", in Korea and Vietnam, before, or even during, the time their men went into battle.

As for our lieutenant, his first instincts were certainly to try to prevent the event the sergeant had advised him was going to happen. Some of us have wondered whether the sergeant may have given the lieutenant a warning not to interfere. At any rate, most of us thought that the incident was one of those battlefield happenings that worked out for the best, given the men and the circumstances involved.

A GI in the mountains above Kiska Harbor, the volcanic cone of Little Kiska Island is in the distance.

A BULLET IN THE BUTT!

After our first Kiska bivouac in rain-filled foxholes, and a long night of distant rifle fire and rumors about the still unseen enemy, we of the Recon swallowed a cold coffee and K-ration breakfast, and joined the lieutenant for orders. While some manned radios, and others patrolled the mountain ridge we were camped on, I was given an intriguing assignment.

"There's a flatland infantry outfit down on the beach," the lieutenant began. " They've never seen a mountain, so they're refusing to climb the one in front of them! Parker, you're to go down, demonstrate that you've already climbed to the top, and lead them to their assigned sector!"

Wondering how the hell I, still a private first class, was going to lead a regiment up the mountain, I saluted, grabbed my helmet and carbine and started back down to the rocky cove where we had landed.

"Report to a colonel so-and-so!" the lieutenant shouted as I left. "If I ever find the damn outfit," I thought, as I picked my way down the steep slope into the thick fog that obscured everything.

But gravity and a vague memory of the terrain led me straight down to Gertrude Cove, from where I picked my way along the beach through a tangle of men, vehicles and equipment until I arrived, unmistakably, at the reluctant infantry outfit. There must have been several hundred sullen soldiers, a gaggle of frustrated officers and piles of rain-soaked equipment spread along the rocky beach. Above them in the fog loomed the mountain the soldiers wouldn't climb.

I approached the angry-looking colonel who seemed in charge and saluted.

"Pfc. Parker, Headquarters 87th reporting," I said. "You sent for a guide?"

The colonel looked curiously at me . Clearly, he had expected someone with more rank, and more apparent leadership status.

"You've been up and down that mountain already?" he asked.

"Yes, sir. It's not nearly as difficult as it looks."

"You know the way to our sector?" he continued.

"Yes sir, if you'll just let me look at your map, and your coordinates."

We briefly studied his map, so I could understand the way the terrain in front of us connected with the 87th's unit locations. I pointed these out to him, then handed back the map.

"I'm ready, if you are, sir." I said.

The colonel's voice was surprisingly big for a smallish man.

"I want everyone's attention" he hollered, and strode down to the edge of the ocean. With his back to the small waves that licked at the sand and rocks, he drew his .45 and held it high over his head.

See This Pistol?

"Everybody see this pistol?" Now he had their attention, the only sounds other than his voice were the waves, and the distant mutter of landing craft engines. "This soldier here," he continued, "is from the 87th Infantry. He and all his buddies have already climbed to the summit ridge of these mountains, and spent the night. He came down this morning at my request!"

His soldiers stared at me, and I heard a muttered "So what is he, a fuckin' hero?"

The colonel's ears were as sharp as mine. "No, he's not a fuckin' hero, he's just a pfc doing his job! Which, by the way, means climbing this mountain again!"

Now he really had their attention. With a gesture of his .45, he waved me up the slope until I stood above all of his men.

Get Ready to Climb!

"When I give the order, this outfit is gonna' follow this soldier until we all get to the ridgeline assigned to us! Get up off your asses, and get ready to climb!"

Grumbling, his men stood, slung on their packs, and picked up their weapons, clearly unhappy with their predicament. But I doubt they guessed what would happen next.

"This is not a goddamn maneuver!" he hollered. "This is war! Our orders are to occupy that ridge, which is what we're gonna do! Any questions?"

Except for a few barely audible mutterings, there were none. His next move surprised all of us. With obvious satisfaction, the colonel released the .45's safety, and then with a loud click, slid back then released the breech, loading a live bullet into the chamber.

Waving the weapon again above his head, the colonel finished his speech. "I'm gonna follow you up this mountain," he shouted. "Anybody doesn't want to climb is gonna get a bullet in his butt, and I mean exactly that!"

With that he spoke quietly to his officers, who each quietly gave their orders to move out. Climbing slowly, aware that the guys following me were carrying full combat gear, I began the long slog upwards. Looking back, I could see the spunky colonel, occasionally waving his .45. His men, intent on the steep grass and rocks, were not about to challenge their leader with a loaded pistol.

The rest of the day was anti-climax. After a long scramble, the men behind me reached their ridge, and deployed along it like the soldiers they really were. Without as much as a "thank you," or a "well done," the colonel asked, "You know your way from here?"

When I answered "Yes, sir!", he turned his back and went about his business, a full 24 hours after he was to have occupied that ridge. Back at 87th headquarters, after a scary but uneventful ramble through the all pervading fog, I reported to the lieutenant.

"Everything go all right?" he queried, and when I said yes, that's all I heard from him. My buddies were full of questions about my assignment. But as far as I know, nothing on the official record of the Kiska campaign ever mentioned the strange story of the reluctant regiment, and the colonel's threat about "a bullet in the butt!"

Ready to overnight in pup tents. Snow dusted Kiska
Volcano is in the background.

PLANKED SALMON AND THE TELLER MINE

We had come down out of the thick fog that shrouded the mountain ridges, the same thick fog through which our riflemen, seeing only distant ghosts, had fired at, and killed, one another. We had been sent on armed patrol to find if any of those ghosts were actually Japanese soldiers, or if, as headquarters now suspected, the Japanese had left Kiska Island more secretly than the U.S. military had believed possible.

Cautiously, in combat formation, we descended the rugged shoulders of the mountain onto rolling tundra slopes that stretched down to the rocky shores of the North Pacific. Packing the 50-pound bulk of my radio, I had to step carefully over the spongy tundra grass while straining my eyes ahead for any sign of the enemy. But as we got closer and closer to Kiska Harbor, it was increasingly evident that, as our cynical song would later chronicle, there were "No Japs at All" on Kiska

Island.

First, it was empty gun emplacements where anti-aircraft cannon barrels pointed toward the empty sky. Then, empty wooden buildings, and the steel-gray waters of the harbor, empty of any ships except the rusty hull of a bombed freighter tilted on its side on an invisible reef.

"Hold up a minute," the lieutenant said, the emptiness and quiet of the place forcing him to keep his voice low. "Let's radio headquarters before going any further."

So I swung the radio to the ground, switched it on, and handed the mike to the lieutenant. "Harbor patrol to headquarters!" His voice sounded as unsteady as we all felt.

"Go ahead, patrol!" The colonel's voice echoed overly loud in the eerie silence. Then the lieutenant in a few words described what we had found.

"Ten-four, patrol," the radio squawked. "Be careful down there. Watch out for booby traps and mines. We'll join you in the morning."

We were left, twenty nervous soldiers, alone among the gun emplacements, buildings, wrecked vehicles and military litter of a major, though abandoned, Japanese harbor and headquarters facility. After a cautious reconnaissance of a few of the wooden barrack buildings, the lieutenant held up his hand.

"It's getting late. We could blow ourselves up, messing around in the dark. Let's get down to the beach, put out guards, and try to get some food and some sleep!"

On the beach, four guys were posted as guards and the rest of us suddenly felt as if we'd been given weekend leave. Corporal Sorenson, one of our Norwegian ski jumpers, knew exactly what to do with our leave time.

Build a Big Fire

"Some of you fellas collect some dry driftwood and build a big fire over against dat bank," Sorenson announced. "Ve're going to have some baked salmon like you've never had before!" Then he took off his shoes and socks, rolled up his pants and told Hawk and me to come along with him.

Mystified, we shed our footwear, hiked up our pants, and waded behind Sorenson into the shockingly cold North Pacific shallows. Then almost magically, we were surrounded by huge fish, seemingly thousands of them, jostling against our legs, and splashing their big tails as they crowded over a shallow sand bar, into the deeper water of a small river's estuary. It was the life-ending spawning run for these salmon, but Sorenson would have to tell us about that later.

Stopping in the midst of this finny horde, Sorenson grinned at our obvious astonishment. "Now here's vat ve do. See how many of dese fish are already dying - dere skin is coming off - de're finished! But see, others, like this guy, de're still solid and firm. Now, vatch!"

With one swift move he stooped, grabbed a big silvery fish, and threw it onto the sandy shore. Almost without stopping, he grabbed and threw another. "I've got to take care of dese fish," he laughed. "Let's see how you guys can do!"

Then Hawk Succeeded

Well, we both tried several times, and failed, to snare our fish. Then Hawk succeeded, with a triumphant grunt, to throw a shimmering salmon to the shore, then I followed with another. "Two more," Sorenson hollered. "Then, ve have enough!"

So we found two more solid specimens, each of them over three feet long, threw them ashore, and waded out onto the cold sand. Sorenson had killed and gutted his catch, and stood holding them, a finger of each hand hooked under their gills.

"My knife's sticking in dat log. Kill and gut your fish, and bring dem along. I'll send somevon to help."

Luckily, Hawk was a fisherman back home, so between us we got the bloody job done. Scandinavians always seem to have one of those Finnish knives, sharp as razors, and Sorenson's was one of the best. With the help of O'Brien, we hauled the fish to the fire, where a cheerful firelit drama was in progress.

Sorenson: Major Domo

By this time, the entire platoon was clustered around in the gathering darkness. Sorenson was acting as cook, fire boss and all-around major domo. On a big driftwood plank, he had fileted his fish with a borrowed knife, thoroughly rinsing them in the nearby salt water. On another plank, he had shown his helpers how to pin filets to the wood with big splinters or old nails found in the driftwood. As we arrived, he was lifting, with a helper, the plank with two-foot long filets, into position against the low bank, directly facing the red-hot fire.

"Dere," he said proudly. "Planked salmon!" (he said "sall-mon!".) You guys keep 'em moist with salt water, and ve'll have the best dom' fish you ever ate!"

Since we had been subsisting on K-rations for four days, the salmon didn't have to be all that good from our point of view. But it was delicious! Sorenson had turned each filet once, so the two inch salmon steaks were thoroughly cooked. We broke off steaming chunks with our fingers, and salted and peppered them to taste from the packets in our K-rations.

Bottles of Saki

One of the guys, unbeknownst to us, had discovered several bottles of Japanese saki in a barracks cupboard, and now generously passed them around from his pack. Salmon, and saki, and the warmth of the fire soon convinced us it was sack time. Spreading our sleeping bags as close to the dying fire as possible, those of us not selected for guard duty were soon snoring, peacefully unaware of the danger lurking beneath our feet.

The next morning was hectic. Before dawn, Navy LST's and small frigates were crowding into the harbor from the other, invasion side of the island, preceded by outboard-driven rubber rafts, manned by demolition teams looking for mines. From the mountains, columns of infantry and engineers streamed in, and began a systematic reconnaissance of the harbor facilities.

After a breakfast of cold salmon and K-ration coffee, we packed our gear, found a spot out of the way of the swarming Army, Navy and CB personnel, and waited for our next orders.

Noticing a team of engineers on the beach, I wandered down to watch. One of them, sweeping the sand with a metal detector with earphones, had stopped suddenly, right above the location of our last night's bonfire. Spotting me, he gestured me nearer.

"Know who built this fire?" he questioned. "We did," I replied. "87th Recon. Had a great salmon roast last night - best food in months! We were the guys... "

Slowly, the engineer backed away from fire site, gesturing for me to be silent. Stripping off his earphones, he lay down the detector and pulled his bayonet out of its scabbard. Returning to the fire, he knelt down gingerly, and began probing the sand and ash with the bayonet.

"Better get well back," he hollered. "You might not be so lucky, this time!

Intrigued, I watched as he probed in an ever wider circle. Then setting aside his bayonet, he started scooping away the sand with his bare hands. Finally satisfied, he sat back on his haunches and signaled me to come down.

While I had been watching, others had gathered to see what was going on. So we filed down to the beach, and stood around in a circle, staring at the ominous object the engineer had unearthed.

Teller Mine

As I remember, it was a mostly black, shiny plastic and metal disc, perhaps two feet across. Our platoon sergeant spoke first. "Teller mine," he breathed. "Jesus! We built the fire right over it!"

The engineer had been watching us. "Yep, it's a Teller mine, and a big mother besides! You know why it didn't explode?"

58

"I suppose it's pressure activated?" the sergeant guessed.

"Yep, explodes from the pressure of a vehicle driving over it. Set here on the beach to destroy a landing craft, or a vehicle being landed from an LCT." He laughed. "Good thing you guys are infantry!"

"But why didn't the heat of the fire set it off?" the sergeant insisted.

"Guess you guys are just lucky. Should have gone off with that much heat!"

After marking the mine with stakes and colored tape for the disposal crew, the engineer donned his headphones, picked up his detector, and resumed his scanning of the beach. We all wandered back to our gear, each guy shaking his head over our near disaster.

It would be more than thirty years before even the smell of cooking salmon didn't remind me of our close call, back in '43, with the planked salmon and the Teller mine.

Kiska tent city, before the wiliwaws blew it down.

Stranded on Kiska

There were no Japanese soldiers on Kiska. As soon as that fact was known, General Corlett's and Admiral Kinkaid's huge armada disappeared over the horizon, leaving the 87th stranded on Kiska.. Until December of 1943, when we were rescued by a ragged flotilla of available shipping, we managed to survive by performing daily patrols, construction and other routine tasks, and by a series of slap-dash but sometimes amusing and exciting "field expedients". And, oh yes, some of us took to writing poems: "Winter's here, the snow is falling - Can't those transports hear us calling?"

KISKA, CLEANLINESS AND
A HOME MADE SAUNA

One our most worrisome problems on Kiska, besides wind, rain and cold, was trying to stay clean in the face of the grimy life style we were living.

There were no workable hot showers on our part of the island, and those outdoor contraptions rigged by inventive GIs were seldom used because of the bitter weather. So we took spit baths, and only occasionally bathed naked in the cold Pacific, or in one of the arctic tarns that dotted the high tundra around camp, in order to stay reasonably clean.

Until, that is, one of our clever Scandinavians said "Why don't we build a sauna?"

In 1943, most of us non-Scandinavian Americans had never even heard of a sauna, say nothing of using one. But we were game to learn, and soon, directed by a Swede, a Finn and a Norwegian, we began scrounging for the materials they prescribed for our sauna.

Their list, it seemed, was endless, but at last we had a pile of materials stacked at the site they chose. This was a sheltered bench, just yards from one of those icy tarns, this one just below our regimental tent city. There were logs, boards, timbers from a nearby Japanese tunnel, copper tubing from the Jap ship wrecked in the harbor, a stove, a pile of fist-sized cobbles from the beach, even some galvanized roofing from one of the bomb-shattered Japanese barracks.

In what seemed no time at all, our Nordic architects had fashioned a small low hut, covered over atop the tin roofing with turf, from which protruded the stove pipe from the undoubtedly illegally obtained Sibley stove.

Inside we found they had built two crude benches to sit on, and encased the stove in a larger metal barrel filled with the rounded stones, atop a bed of cobbles. A copper pipe led from a water barrel, wrapped tightly around the stove, and ended in a spigot suspended over the stones. Next to the stove a bucket full of coal needed no explanation.

Our Finnish expert outlined how the equipment would be used. "First, ve heat up the stove, and the rocks around. Hot vater from the pipe drops on the rocks and makes steam. If ve vant more steam, ve dip this dipper in the vater barrel, and throw cold vater on the rocks. It's a good sauna, almost as good as back home!"

And so it was, as soon as we figured out how to close tightly the rather rickety door. We all got a chance to sit, and sweat, and clean off with a brush and soap, then run outside and rinse off in the water of the tarn. And we had the sauna all to ourselves, until word got around how effective it was.

The Officers Have Heard

One day our platoon sergeant got us together in one of our big pyramidal tents. "I hate to tell you this," he began, "but the officers have heard about our sauna."

There was general silence in the tent. We all thought we knew what was coming.

"It's not all that bad," he went on. "All they want is a special time for officers in the sauna - the rest of the time is ours!"

There was an instant hubbub of voices, then one of the Scandinavian sauna architects hollered for silence.

"Dat's OK," he said, so long as our times are evenings, ven our duties are over!"

The sergeant, somewhat taken aback by the chorus of voices that supported the sauna expert, held up his hands in acquiescence.

"OK," he responded. "I'll try to arrange it your way!"

And that's the way it worked out. A list of times was posted on the sauna door, with late afternoon and evening preference given, for a change, to the enlisted men.

I asked the Swedish sauna builder what he would have done, if the officers hadn't acceded to his request.

"You know," he grinned. "Dot copper pipe was the last one on Kiska. Vitout it, it vouldn't have been much of a sauna!"

With that, he grabbed his towel, and headed out to our sauna for another good sweat. By the time we left Kiska, we were, including the officers, the cleanest outfit on the island.

THE ULTIMATE OUTHOUSE

Kiska, and the Aleutians in general, are internationally known for their williwaw winds. At our regimental enclave, we had to string climbing ropes between tents, just to move anywhere against the wind. One day I wheedled an extra cup of coffee from the mess sergeant, and clinging to a rope, I hadn't gone ten feet before the wind had sucked all the coffee from my deep canteen cup. Even more irritating, when I got back to my tent, my cup was not only empty, but was dry as a bone! All of our tents, by now, had been dug deeply into the volcanic soil, after an earlier storm had blown down the entire city of tents we had built during the first days on the island.

So you should be able to sympathize with the unfortunate soldier who had to relieve his bowels by squatting over an open slit trench in a typical fifty or sixty-miles-per-hour williwaw wind. We tried putting up wind screens of posts and canvas, but these regularly blew away. We sought out surface depressions in which to dig our trenches, but these only helped a little during a normal twenty or thirty mile-an-hour wind.

It got so that most of us waited to empty our bowels (if we could) for the few calm days that came along between storms. Until, that is, one of our resident Edisons awoke with a light bulb over his head and announced his plan for a williwaw-proof outhouse!

To escape the deadly bombs that the U.S. Navy and Air Force rained on Kiska prior to the invasion, the Japanese troops, like organized moles, had dug miles of timber-supported tunnels throughout the largely vol-canic-ash hills and ridges around the harbor area. Our Edison knew, as did we all, that a large tunnel entrance lay just below our company bivouac area. Why not build a company outhouse within that entrance, completely sheltered from the winds that had plagued us for weeks?

No sooner said than done. Receiving top priority for the project, our carpenters requisitioned scarce lumber from the island quartermaster, nails and screws, canvas and even some olive drab paint. Almost overnight, a pristine four-holer was built in the tunnel entrance, perched over a deep trench, dug in the soft ash of course by we members of the "other ranks", as the British would say. A clever shield of staggered canvas walls provided privacy.

Our Company Crapper

The morning after it was finished, the new facility was first used by three officers, who had assured their priority by posting a sign at the door establishing hours of use for our company "crapper". Inevitably, officers took precedence during post-breakfast and supper hours. The rest of us had to wait for a convenient break during the day.

So it went for a few weeks, all of us adjusting our bowel movements to the schedule on the door. On windy days, the outhouse was one of the few quiet spots on the island; a blessed relief after our earlier slit-trench adventures.

Meanwhile, unbeknownst to us, another series of events linked to the Japanese tunnels was occurring just over the "outhouse hill" from our company area. There, the CO of an engineer company had discovered that several of his soldiers were using the network of tunnels to disappear into, to avoid whatever disagreeable "details" they might have been assigned. Within the tunnels, they located cozy rooms, where they stashed food, smokes and even lanterns and candles by which to read whatever paperbacks they could find.

Incensed by this malingering, the captain decided to take definitive action. Quietly, he gathered his demolition experts, dynamite and primacord, and laid explosive charges at the entrances to every tunnel on his side of our outhouse hill.

Next, he sent runners to every unit on his side, warning all they'd better be out of the tunnels by 8:30 hours next morning. Word spread fast; nobody wanted to be in one of those tunnels when the dynamite exploded and the tunnels were closed! Unfortunately, he forgot to notify our outfit on the other side of the hill!

Following their usual schedule, some of our officers enjoyed breakfast next morning, then retired with the usual reading matter to our luxurious outhouse. And at precisely 8:30, the engineer captain ordered the demolition of all those offending tunnels just over the hill.

We all heard the explosions, but figured the engineers were, as had been fairly frequent, destroying some abandoned Japanese ordinance. What we didn't know was that at least one tunnel on the other side connected all the way through the hill to the tunnel where we had proudly built our outhouse.

A Hammer of Air

Like water pouring through a culvert, the air in that tunnel, sharply compressed by the explosions, rushed silently, in the only direction it could, towards the unsuspecting officers, seated comfortably on the four-holer. Reaching them with near hurricane force, this hammer of air blew down the outhouse frame, blew the officers off their thrones, and ripped away the canvas screen, depositing all in a jumble of wood, canvas and half-naked officers in the tundra outside. All that remained intact was the woodwork of the four-holer, low and solid enough to avoid the blast!

Fortunately, only the egos of the officers involved

were somewhat damaged. After being assured by the engineers that there would be no more explosions, the colonel authorized our carpenters to reconstruct the facility. Strangely, the schedule notice, formerly posted outside, was never replaced. From that day until we left the island, our ultimate outhouse was utilized by all hands strictly on a "come when you're ready" basis.

NO SKIS FOR SKI TROOPERS

We were, after all, ski troops. And one would expect that ski troops, on a remote Aleutian island, with winter coming on, might be equipped by an all-seeing Army Quartermaster Corps, with skis, and the equipment that should go with them.

But one would be wrong. In fact, except for rubber and leather shoe pacs, wool socks, underwear and pants, relatively wind proof parkas and our mountain caps, we had nothing at all that remotely resembled the superb winter gear that had been issued to us at Camp Hale, Colorado.

And of course, in late November, it began to snow. Not the deep, fluffy powder of high country Colorado. Not even the relatively moist but solidly packed snow of the European Alps. Our Aleutian snow was fine, sparse, and extremely lucky to adhere to the ground at all in the fierce willawaw winds that blew in the Aleutians in winter.

But it was snow, and we were skiers. We went to our supply sergeant, and begged him to canvass the Aleutians and Alaska for some skis. So he got on the radio, and was told, mistakenly it turned out, that the nearest skis might be at Fort Lewis, Washington - 2600 miles away.

Knowing full well that Fort Lewis might as well be Timbuktu as far as the availability of skis was concerned, we turned to our last possible source, the always knowledgeable, always manually skilled Norwegians, Swedes and Finns among us. Could they possibly make some skis for us?

No problem, they agreed. If, and this was a huge if, we could find some wood suitable for skis!

There were three likely sources of wood on Kiska. First, driftwood, the battered, twisted remnants of distant forests we found on the beaches. Second, the wood the Japanese had brought in for their barracks, buildings and underground structures, most of which the CBs and engineers had appropriated for their own uses. And finally, the few thousand feet of building lumber shipped in by the Navy, all of which had been incorporated into the relatively luxurious facilities the Navy had built in the harbor area.

It looked bad for any skis being fashioned by our Scandinavian carpenters. Then one of us, I can't remember who, recalled he'd seen some pine paneling in the officer's mess on the Nozima Maru, the Japanese ship which lay wrecked in the harbor. Maybe some of that wood hadn't been ripped off by one or the other of our voracious materials-scavenging teams.

A group of our carpenter types hitched a ride down to the harbor, and somehow wangled a rubber raft from the CBs. In less than two hours, they were back, having rafted ashore a supply of pine boards (probably originally from Oregon), pried from the walls of the Nozima Maru. Hitching another ride in one of our tracked trailers, pulled behind a small caterpillar tractor, the ski carpenters arrived at the 87th's headquarters area to the cheers of a crowd of eager skiers.

Skiing at Last
Maybe at last we could go skiing on the snowy slopes of Ski Kiska!

Happily, our Scandinavian artisans knew what they were doing. Starting by planing smooth the roughly six-foot-long boards, they next cut mortices through the boards for toe straps.

While one team continued this process, another was steam-softening the v-shaped tips of the boards already prepared, then bending them in a crude vice into the

approximate shape of old-fashioned Norwegian skis.
The final step proved the most difficult. The skis
needed grooves if they were to run at all straight.
Lacking a tool like a router, our frontier carpenters
decided to burn a long straight groove the running
length of each ski with red hot, poker-like steel rods.
Inevitably, these jury-rigged grooves proved anything
but straight. But we had at last, as I remember, four pairs
of quite presentable skis!

Bindings and toe straps of varying effectiveness were
quickly fashioned from the plenitude of canvas and
leather found around every Army facility. When the skis
were ready, our carpenters got first preference, so we all
trooped out to the most viable ski slope, a shallow gully
filled with snow on the hill above camp.

Finally the ski troops were going to ski!

Not surprisingly, after walking to the top, our
Scandinavian carpenters skied relatively gracefully, all
of them using their ancient Telemark turns because of
the looseness of the bindings, the crudeness of the skis,
and the fact they were wearing either GI boots, or snow
pacs!

I don't remember how the skis were waxed - probably with candle-wax. We had plenty of fat paraffin candles as back up illumination for our gas lanterns.

As for the rest of us, the Scandinavians could be
excused for standing aside and smiling politely, as we
snowplowed and stemmed and sitzmarked down the
narrow slope. There was nothing very graceful about
our Army style descents. But at least we were skiing!

K Slope on Kiska

For the remainder of our stay on Kiska, we skiers
took turns with our crude skis, and eventually demonstrated an approximate mastery over our snow-gully ski
hill. As I recall, we named it K-slope, K for Kiska,
remembering A, B and C ski slopes at Camp Hale.

We hadn't been skiing long when our much-delayed
travel orders arrived, and we were soon aboard trans-

ports on our way back to the States. But that wasn't the end of the Ski Kiska story. Many years later, I received a curious phone call. It was another World War II veteran, who had been a medical officer on Adak Island, up the Aleutian chain from Kiska. He had somehow heard I was a ski trooper and got my telephone number from the 10th Mountain Association.

"You guys were ski troops," he began. "Did you ever do any skiing on Kiska?"

I replied by telling him the story of our home-made skis. "We never had any of the winter equipment designed for us back in the States," I said.

A Military Snafu

"No wonder," he laughed. "We had all your equipment! It's a typical story of military snafu, that benefitted us, and royally screwed you guys on Kiska."

It seems the Quartermaster Corps did remember us skiers on Kiska, sometime in the fall of 1943. So they shipped a number of skis, boots and poles, with an additional package of rope ski tow equipment, up the Inland Passage, and out the chain of islands, destination Kiska.

Somewhere along the way, the shipment's waybills were mislaid, so when it reached Adak, the Quartermaster officer there, lacking instructions, simply stored the lot in his warehouse. No one on Adak apparently knew there were skiers on Kiska!

"That's where we came in," chuckled the former medical officer. "A skier myself, when I saw the stored equipment, I thought the guys would enjoy a little winter recreation. So another skier and I set up the rope tow on a nearby slope, and announced the availability, free of charge, of a little winter fun for everyone!"

For the longest time I was silent, blown away by this tale of good intentions gone awry.

"I hope your men had fun," I said, "with the ski gear meant for us!"

He laughed again. "Not many of my medical detachment, or the rest of the guys on the base, took advantage of the free skiing. But I thought you ought to know what happened to all of that great ski equipment!"

Thanking him, I hung up the phone. Maybe some day, I thought, I'll be able to tell this story of the mislaid equipment, and the medical officer, and the home-made skis on Kiska!

A pyramidal tent before being dug in. The artist has exaggerated the size of Little Kiska volcano in the distance.

The Craft That Carried Us From Kiska

When the transports finally arrived, it was our ironic luck to be assigned to the Denali, a side-wheel steamer designed in the 1880's to carry tourists up and down the sheltered waters of British Columbia's and Alaska's Inland Passage. Drawing just eight feet of water under her copper hull, the Denali seemed crowded, but apparently seaworthy. Then we reached the open waters of the Gulf of Alaska.

SIDE-WHEELER IN A STORM

Awed and frightened at the same time, my Navy buddy and I huddled at the forward end of the promenade deck and watched a mountain of gray-green sea water crash over the bow of our frail paddle-wheel steamer, sweep over the fore-deck, and collide with a giant fountain of spray against the wall of the ship's forecastle. It was my first experience with a storm at sea, and the raw images it burned into my brain are, after more than 60 years, still as fresh as they were during that perilous deck watch in the Gulf of Alaska.

Most American soldiers in World War II were transported at sea in relatively new, relatively seaworthy transport ships. But the men of the 87th Mountain Infantry seemed to attract a different kind of transport vessel. In our case, returning from the Aleutian island of Kiska in December, 1943, at least two hundred of us were packed into the venerable steamship Denali, (the Native's name for Mount McKinley) unbelievably, a copper-bottomed wooden sidewheeler that had been operating in the shallow waters of the Alaskan Inland Passage since sometime in the last quarter of the 19th century! Apparently, she was the only craft available during a time of extreme scarcity of transport ships in the Pacific.

As we churned eastward toward the mainland along the Aleutian Island chain, the seas were calm enough so that we could enjoy the incredible Aleutian wildlife. From the decks and portholes we watched sea otters, floating happily on their backs with fat shellfish held on their chests or tummies. Dozens of sea birds; gulls, petrels, kittiwakes and many unknown species swirled around the ship, crying in a dozen bird languages. Dolphins leaped along our bow waves, as if escorting us back to a somewhat safer world.

At night, the black ocean boiling behind us was lit with a stunning array of glowing shapes the sailors said were jellyfish and other, to us, mysterious, phosphorescent denizens of North Pacific waters.

Cruising past Kodiak Island, the last land we'd see for two days, we watched fascinated through our field glasses as giant Kodiak bears ambled through the island's long grasses, apparently the only living things on that desolate shore.

But Kodiak was the end of our ocean idyll. As we left the island astern, the winds increased dramatically, and suddenly a maelstrom of giant waves began to batter our little ship. I should explain that I had volunteered for deck duty, so I had an immediate and frightening introduction to what sailors later told us was the worst winter storm in the Gulf of Alaska in a hundred years!

We had been sailing as part of a troop convoy; two Liberty ships, a modern freighter/troop ship and a destroyer. But as soon as the storm began, we lost sight of the other craft, and were alone in the Gulf until we reached the welcome shelter of Cross Sound. Luckily, we did not know how alone we were, nor how fortunate we were to be on board the Denali, until we heard the terrifying details of the convoy's battle with the storm.

Explaining Deck Duty

Let me explain about deck duty. Because of the Navy's natural fear of Japanese submarines, the North Pacific rule for convoys was "watch on watch." For every Navy deck watchman, they required an Army watchman as well, to keep an eye out for enemy ships, and for any show of tell-tale lights on the ships of the convoy. Because I hated the confinement of the hold, with dozens of men smoking, coughing, being sea-sick or otherwise fouling the air, I had volunteered for the open although sometimes storm-battered life on deck watch.

Even before the storm hit, my Navy partner insisted I don naval storm gear, bulky, warm and nearly water-proof parka and pants, and clip into the safety line that was slung along each exposed deck. Since my watch began just as we encountered the edges of the storm, I lived through what even veteran sailors seldom do, the worst of one of nature's most frightening phenomena, a North Pacific typhoon.

The first, most obvious evidence that the ship might be in trouble was the insistent loud creaking of her wooden joints, a noise that persisted until we were well into the calm waters of the Inland Passage. Built proba-bly in the 1880's, primarily of Sitka spruce and hard-woods, the old vessel literally squeaked and groaned whenever her superstructure was twisted by the growing fury of the storm. And as we pitched and rolled in the waves, we could hear her engine whining extra loudly each time the skipper called on a paddlewheel to work harder.

My immediate, and, as it turned out, my increasing concern, was that this vulnerable craft, designed for calm sheltered waterways, could not possibly be equal to the gigantic strain of fighting this storm. Yet, as I began to be aware, there was something special about our skipper, and about the Denali, that made them as a team more than equal to this challenge.

As my equally worried but more knowledgeable Navy sidekick explained, our sidewheeler had an advantage in a big storm that other ordinary craft did not. All modern ships have both steering (rudders), and power source (propellers) well back towards their sterns. As such craft pitch upward onto the crest of a wave, with both bow and stern projecting out into the air, there is a long moment when the ship has neither power nor steerage.

As a result, the ship's captain is momentarily help-less to line up his ship with the huge storm waves and winds. Many a fine vessel in a truly nasty storm has therefore rolled sidewise into the trough of a great wave and either foundered, or suffered serious damage as she fought to right herself.

The Vertiginous Side

On the Denali, as we labored up the side of a huge wave, our skipper would apply extra power to one pad-dle wheel or the other, so as we topped the wave the ship would be perfectly aligned with the storm's forces. Then our tiny cockle-shell would literally surf down the ver-tiginous windward side of the wave, crash straight on into the next wave, then seem to shake itself, like a wet Labrador retriever, and safely climb the next watery slope.

But except for being aware that our ship seemed to be holding its own, I was far from enjoying the storm. Even though driving spray and rain had reduced our vis-ibility to zero, our Navy bo'sun boss kept us out on deck.

"Ya never know when you guys are gonna' see somp'n they can't see on the bridge!" he said, as he delivered us hot coffee in big Navy mugs. "Hang in there - we should be out of this storm in an hour or so!"

Well, it was more like five or six hours, of two hours on and two off, before the Gulf began to calm down. Meanwhile, both my Navy partner and I were frequent-ly swept off our feet to the end of our lifelines, smoth-ered under errant, ice-cold waves or otherwise remind-ed of the hazards of deck duty in a storm. And we saw nothing, except stinging spray, waves as high as houses, and the slippery wet expanse of our assigned Promenade deck. If this was life in the Navy, I thought, I'm better off in the Infantry!

Finally the wind screaming in the guy wires above decks and the creaking of the ship's wooden joints began to tone down, and the waves, still huge but more regular, quieted so we didn't have to shout to be heard. Relaxing in the Navy mess when our watch was over, the bos'n told us we were entering Cross Sound, and we "watch on watch " people could stand down. After a quick sandwich, I hung up my heavy weather gear and climbed to an upper deck to where my lifeboat sleeping quarters hung in davits.

Images of The Storm
    Relieved that its taut canvas cover had kept the lifeboat dry, I unlashed the canvas and crawled into my sleeping bag, cushioned on life belts. For a long time stark images of the storm kept me awake, then sheer exhaustion took over. When I awoke and crawled out into the sunshine, I could hardly believe the placid, unruffled waters of the Inland Passage. Glacier-hung mountains filled the eastern skyline, and friendly sea birds again circled our ship.
    Memories of that great storm might have faded quickly, if we hadn't heard how the rest of the convoy had fared. One of the Liberty ships had broken in two in the trough of a giant wave. If the Liberty ship had not been designed with separate floating sections, and if the Navy rescue operation had been less professional, many of our men might have drowned. As it was, not a man was lost, though the convoy didn't reach its destination, Ketchikan, until we had already departed on an east-bound troop train.
    Many of my wartime Navy friends have a hard time believing my tales of adventures at sea - few if any of them experienced the fury of nature we felt in the Gulf of Alaska. Maybe I was lucky, 90 days at sea, in the Infantry, and I never saw an enemy ship! It has occurred to me, I ought to have a Navy ribbon to add to my Combat Infantry array. Then maybe people would have to believe sea stories like this one - the unlikely story of the craft Denali, the old side-wheeler that steamed us safely through the great storm of '43.

Ski troopers in winter whites march down
a company street at Camp Hale.

Work and Play at Camp Hale

*Returned from the Aleutians, once again we sea-level sol-
diers had to adjust to life above 9,200 feet at Camp Hale.
After a long train trip from Alaska and a strange, barracks-
bound Christmas, we began mountain training with a
vengeance, packing a year of ordinary activity into five strenuous months. There were a few exciting weekends at nearby
ski towns, hot springs resorts, or an occasional trip to the big
city of Denver (Population: 350,000). But mostly it was cold
and snowy, or muddy and slippery, and always steep and
rocky while we really learned the skills of a mountain soldier.*

UP RESOLUTION CREEK WITH
PACK AND GUN

We were supposed to be "ski troops." Photos in national magazines and in newsreel films showed some of us swooping down the slopes of Cooper Hill or throwing up rooster tails of powder snow off of alpine precipices.

But the reality was far different. Once we had learned, as a company, how to ski reasonably well at Cooper Hill, the emphasis shifted. Now it was physical and tactical training, in company units. And most of this took place on the snowy peaks up Resolution Creek.

Of course we had regimental and division-size maneuvers, like the first and second Homestake Peak exercises and the D-Series. We suffered through long, cold, windy hours on the rifle range and the live ammo combat course and the bayonet course and the machine gun and mortar ranges. The sometimes dangerous and always tough and dirty work tending our cantankerous beasts of burden at "mule school." The rock climbing drills on the 14th Street rocks, the mountain combat course and the artificial glacier for ice climbing. But some of our more sadistic senior officers had decided we needed more conditioning, with full packs, mountain gear, guns and skis. The best place for this, they decided, was up the Resolution Creek road.

Some weeks, it happened daily. After reveille and breakfast, we'd fall out in the company street by platoons. A sergeant would check to see we had thirty pound packs, rifles (or other weapons), proper winter clothing, dark glasses and skis, skins, poles and boots. Satisfied, he would report "All present and accounted for, sir!" The company would then march, "right shoulder, skis!" the mile or so north on mud or gravel until we reached the packed snow of the Resolution Creek road. Then the real work began.

Mounting Skins

We quickly mastered the tricky ritual of mounting our climbing skins on the soles of our clumsy, seven-foot-long skis. Without sticky wax on the slick bottoms of the skis, the skins slipped off with exasperating frequency as we climbed. So our knowledgeable Scandinavian companions taught us how to wax for holding skins in place, then to rewax for the downhill slide. After our first clumsy efforts, we were soon ready for whatever the day would bring.

Resolution Creek valley rises from 9,200 feet at Camp Hale to 11,200 feet at timberline, over perhaps two or two and a half miles of steep, variable snow. We usually climbed for two hours and took two ten-minute breaks before we reached the day's exercise location. Then platoons would split up, climb to locations on Ptarmigan or Resolution or Sugarloaf or Pearl Peaks, all of them near or over 12,000 feet above sea level, and begin the exercise for the day.

Sometimes these mini-maneuvers were fun; quick climbs, then an exhilarating slide on skis to ambush an entrenched enemy. Sometimes they were endless waits in a cold snow foxhole until we too became the defeated adversary. Daily lunch was cold C-rations, or even at times the much-maligned K-rations; an energy bar, crackers, cheese, chocolate, coffee and a cigarette. If you ran out of the water in your canteen, the limitless fields of snow around you were not yet so polluted that you didn't dare eat snow!

After three or four hours of exercises, there was the long, snaking return on skis, first on open slopes, then through the spruce and fir forests, then in a perpetual snowplow behind the guy in front for the last 1,000 feet down the road to the end of the snow. The next day, like as not, we had to do it again. Not exactly glamorous skiing!

Camp Hale looking north, home for 15,000 soldiers.
Resolution Creek is at the upper middle right of the photo.

Several times the drill was a two or three day overnight, and these were more fun. We carried heavier packs, with tents, sleeping bags and mountain rations for our meals; large cans of bacon, dried eggs, spam, dried potatoes and vegetables, and occasionally the always popular syrupy fruit cocktail. If the cooks were in a good mood, they'd throw in some cans of jam, and loaves of bread to be toasted over our open fires.

Somehow these mini-maneuvers were more imaginative. One exercise had some of us skiing over firm spring snow by moonlight, to attack a unit camped on the opposite side of Sugarloaf Peak. Skiing from moonlight into shadow was like entering a carnival spook house - we slid from darkness to light to darkness, depending on limber knees and strong legs to adjust as we glided in varying light over uncertain terrain. The added thrill of cutting tent ropes, and awakening our "enemies" with the points of our bayonets made this maneuver almost as real, without the danger, as our later patrols experienced at night in Italy.

Patrols on Skis
When our captain ran out of ideas on these longer trips, we'd split up into patrols on skis. I remember climbing to the ridge above Ptarmigan Pass, and out of sight of our officers, practicing terrain jumps off a giant wind cornice onto spring corn snow. Then returning, we linked stem christies down through perfect powder snow, preserved by the altitude and the steep north-facing tilt of Ptarmigan Peak.

Though we always had to carry our heavy, inefficient "mountain tents" on these overnights, most of us erected them somewhere in plain sight, then sought out a snow cave under a big spruce, built a floor of spruce boughs, and spent the night there in natural comfort. After the first "tents by the numbers" efforts by our officers, it was they, and only they, who slept in those miserable, frost bedeviled shelters.

Unhindered by official protocol, however, the officers never hesitated to join us around our big squad-size bonfires, where we cooked supper, then drank coffee, ate toast and jam, and sang mountain songs into the night. If there was a bright side to our Resolution Creek labors, it was these hours around the fire, where rank and privilege were, at least temporarily, forgotten.

Hard, Dirty Work
But mostly, Resolution Creek was hard, dirty work. Sweating in the sun, freezing if you stopped in shadow. Eye-piercing brightness from the high altitude sun, in spite of the clumsy Army-issue dark goggles. The constant, shoulder and back-straining weight of pack and rifle and other gear. The endless lifting of one boot and ski, followed by another and another, up 2,000 vertical

feet and two horizontal miles, all above 9,200 feet in Colorado's high, dry air. Then the irritating accordion on skis, as we slid one behind the other back to camp.

In the final analysis, however, our officers were right. The many hours we spent on Resolution Creek, plus all the other muscle and endurance-building activities our Camp Hale training entailed resulted in a group of men in fabulous physical shape.

When German officers marveled to see American GI's attacking on the run up the steep slopes of the Apennines, it was legs and lungs developed on Camp Hale's slopes and trails that made the difference. Whether we were better soldiers is debatable. But that we were in the best condition of any American soldiers in Italy is not. Our mountain training prepared us for mountain combat. And the tiresome but muscle-building trail up Resolution Creek, after all, must have helped the 10th Mountain Division through its four bitter months of war.

At least, in retrospect, I like to think it did.

Aspen in 1948. The zig-zag trail to the right of the white lift line is the Corkscrew section of the old Roch Run.

THE MIDNIGHT MINE RUN

One of the rarest treats we ski-troopers in training enjoyed while at Camp Hale was a weekend in Aspen, including a trip down the Roch Run. Such a weekend started in someone's old vehicle, running on gas bought with rationed coupons. No one dared ask how the coupons were acquired.

Leaving Hale at five o'clock on the dot, we'd drive to Glenwood Springs, have a steak or pork chop at a local restaurant and arrive in Aspen after dark, with the black and white outlines of Aspen Mountain looming above the town. A bed in the Jerome hotel was a dollar, or five bucks for two if you shared the bridal suite with another guy.

Next morning, on one memorable weekend, our gang of eager ski troopers wolfed down a hearty Jerome breakfast (50 cents, and all you could eat), and hurried outside so we wouldn't miss the mine truck. In those days, if you wanted to ski the Roch Run, you climbed the 2,000 vertical feet to its start on an old mine road, or you rode the truck to the Midnight Mine. So we waited in the cold dawn until a rattle-trap truck pulled up outside the Jerome front door.

After greeting the driver and another miner in the cab, we tossed our skis and packs among the cables, shovels and other mine equipment, climbed after our gear, and tried to find someplace comfortable amidst the cold steel tools and bulky skis and poles.

Ski troopers Kasabuski, Wigdahl, Parker and Landry atop Aspen Mountain - circa 1943-44.

One remembers little about that excruciatingly cold drive. We followed the Castle Creek road to the mine cutoff, then, the truck in low-low gear, switched back and forth up the long climb to the mine. Half frozen, we tumbled off the truck in the mine parking lot, thanked the driver, retrieved our gear and began strapping on our climbing skins for the remaining trek to the top of Richmond Hill. The ensuing climb on skins slowly revived our circulation and our spirits, so that topping out on the ridge we were finally ready for the adventure ahead.

Richmond Hill

Richmond Hill is the old name for the long ridge that culminates at today's gondola terminal and the Sun-Deck restaurant. With our climbing skins off and stowed away, and binding cables still set for cross country, we glided north along the ridge, taking in the glorious scenery across the Roaring Fork valley. This was why each one of us had joined the ski troops - fresh powder snow, and the mountain world to ourselves!

At a point close to the top of today's Ruthie's ski lift, we stopped to tighten our binding cables and slip on our parkas. From here on, it was downhill all the way! One of us who knew the way led off down today's Buckhorn slope in trackless powder. We followed, someone yodeling to express the joy everyone felt. Turn after turn, in those days mostly stem-christies, until at the bottom of Buckhorn our leader swished to a stop and hollered - "Time for lunch!"

And what a place for lunch! On a bench that terminated in a rocky crag, we sat on our skis, ate sandwiches provided by Mrs. Elisha at the Jerome, and took in the scenery. Directly across Castle Creek loomed snow-draped Highland Peak. Partly hidden behind Highland ridge, craggy Castle Peak. Further south the imposing mass of Mount Hayden. If there is a mountain trooper's heaven, this is what it would look like!

The Precipitous Corkscrew

But we were there for the skiing, so we were soon sliding along the road that tops Tourtellot Park, to stop again at the future site of old Lift Number One's upper terminal. This was the real beginning of the Roch Run. Anticipating the precipitous Corkscrew soon to come, we again checked our bindings, and made sure packs and gear were secure. Some of us New Englanders, never having skied a mountain this imposing, experienced the same gut-tightening feeling we had felt before our first ride on a big Ferris wheel or roller coaster. But we were all game, so off we went, down what is now upper Ruthie's into Zogg Park, still in flawless powder, and across the park to the mouth of the Corkscrew. Here began the real test! Swiss ski and mountaineering pioneer Andre Roch had surveyed the Roch Run around the winter of 1935-36, and local ski enthusiasts cut the trail during subsequent summers. Following the traditions of the times, the Corkscrew, a steep, twisting wiggle of a trail through thick woods, was cut scarcely 20 yards wide! But not knowing any better, we launched ourselves one at a time into the Corkscrew as if it were just a part of one of our skiing tests back at Camp Hale.

Many a Sitzmark

After many a sitzmark and a few somersaults on skis, we emerged on the road at the base of Corkscrew. Now below us spread the checkerboard pattern of Aspen in 1944 - dozens of empty, snow-covered building-lots, and a few pioneer buildings still standing, the Jerome, the Opera House and the Red Onion among them. We stopped to take in the view and brush off some of the potentially embarrassing snow built up on our packs and clothes. Feeling like conquering heroes, we skied down to the Ski Club shack for a couple of rides up on the boat tow and down the Club practice slope. Then, sliding across several snow-covered streets and vacant lots, we stacked our skis outside the Jerome bar and kicked the snow off our boots.

It was time for an Aspen Crud (or two) in the bar and an enthusiastic retelling of our adventure, before a nourishing supper (75 cents, $1.25 for a steak) in the dining room. How many of today's skiers, 60 years later, will remember a day of skiing as simple, satisfying, and exciting as the one we enjoyed on Aspen Mountain, in 1944?

Members of the Recon platoon on their bridge, built during training at Camp Hale in the spring of 1944. The lieutenant is second from left.

Camp Swift - Texas?

Incredibly, our seesaw, high-altitude/low altitude careers continued. In early summer, we again left our happy home at Camp Hale and entrained for Camp Swift, Texas. Justification for the move was that we needed joint training with tank and other flatland weapons units. But the heat, snakes, bugs and other crawling things of Texas soon had many men wanting to transfer out. D-day in France had come and gone, yet we still hadn't really seen mountain warfare.

Those of us in Recon, however, got a lucky break. While our line company buddies slogged over the dusty, muddy acres of central Texas on foot, frequently leading mules, we, like old-time cavalry, rode horseback everywhere. But it was still Texas, not the Alps!

THE MULES OF BASTROP COUNTY

Never mind why we mountain troopers were in Texas. There we were, in Camp Swift, near Bastrop, Texas, and one part of our "mission" was to learn more about coordinating our mule pack artillery with our new expanded infantry division status. So they sent to Fort Riley, Kansas for more mules. Several hundred more! We of the Recon platoon already had our horses, and we were busy in the pitiless Texas sun shoveling manure, grooming our mounts and tidying up our picket line area when we got new orders. "Report to the rail head for mule duty." So we formed up in a loose platoon formation and ambled down to where a spur of the railroad ended in the center of camp.

I should explain here that most of us relatively veteran members of the 10th had already had required mule training at Camp Hale. Our leaders felt we should all be able to help our pack artillery men with their mules when the occasion demanded. So we had learned to water, groom, harness and lead the artillery mules (and avoid those wicked hooves!)

However, many of the newer men in the outfit had never had such training, Therein lay the problem with the newly arriving Fort Riley mules.

At the rail head, several boxcar loads of animals had already arrived, drawn up alongside wooden unloading ramps. The routine looked simple; hitch a rope to each mule's hackamore, or halter, lead it down the ramp, then lead it the waiting picket lines. Our platoon sergeant reported to the nearest officer, and we almost immediately went to work.

For us, in spite of an occasional recalcitrant animal, it was a routine task. Some mules had to be bodily shoved out of the boxcar by the sweating artillerymen in charge. Others tried to bite or kick the guys leading them, but by and large each boxcar was emptied with only minor incidents.

Kicking Its Heels

But that was not the case at other unloading ramps. We first became aware of the problem when a mule with flying rope and no soldier attached ran bucking past us in a swirl of Texas dust. Then another mule, dragging a soldier, ran sidewise past, finally rid itself of its "keeper," and kicking its heels gleefully disappeared after its mate.

In the next hour or so, similar scenes were repeated all over the unloading area. The stubborn but intelligent animals, apparently sensing their advantage over the untrained soldiers, pulled, yanked or jerked themselves free, then followed one another in every direction but toward the waiting picket lines. Many mules couldn't wait for the halter ropes, crowded out of the confining boxcars, down the ramps and galloped away wearing just their U.S. Army hackamores and, witnesses claimed, supercilious grins on their faces!

We more experienced GI's, and the sweating, swearing artillerymen, helped where we could. But when the rail head dust finally settled, and most of the mules had been cornered, then tied up to their picket lines, several dozen animals were still missing.

In succeeding days, many of the escapees were rounded up, most of them waiting docilely in farmer's corrals or barns scattered over the Texas countryside. But when the 10th left Camp Swift for Italy in the fall, there was still a bunch of Army mules unaccounted for.

According to division lore, it was soon known all over central Texas that quite a few farmers and ranchers in the area owned large, well-muscled mules, somewhat superior in physique and training to the general run of Texas mules. And when a big strong mule would show up for sale at a livestock auction, a prospective buyer would look the other way when it came time to examine its brand.

Both seller, and buyer, would smile, and maybe the buyer would say, "Damn good lookin' animal. Must be one a' them Bastrop County mules!"

Mules and men readying for a long hot march
in the sun at Camp Swift, Texas.

BIG RED AND THE HORSE WHISPERER

When we of the Recon platoon first got our horses at Camp Swift, Texas, in the summer of 1944, none of us had ever heard of anyone like today's "horse whisperers." Our heroes were those rough and ready cowboys who "broke" wild horses in the old way, by riding them 'til their spirits were broken. Little did we know that an old cowhand among us might have been one of the first of those horsemen who "broke" horses by out-thinking and out-guessing them in a truly amazing way. This is the story of Bill Kettley, an ex-cowboy from Wyoming, and the horse we thought no one could ride.

In the first place, it was a truly crazy idea to try to turn mountain Recon platoons into horse cavalry units. But some old cavalry colonel, in spite of the horrendous tales we all had heard about the destruction of crack Polish cavalry squadrons by German Panzers, decided we mountain troopers might someday have to fight on horseback. So he ordered a bunch of rough-broke horses from Fort Riley, Kansas. When we got to Camp Swift from the mountains of Colorado, on almost the first day they called us in and told us we were going to be horse-mounted cavalry!

Luckily, because some of our old-timers had been in the horse cavalry, or were experienced pack guides or mule skinners, we had a reasonably expert cadre. Their first problem was to gentle our string of half-broke remount horses enough so the rest of us could ride them. Their second was to teach us skiers and mountain climbers how to ride!

As it turned out, with the guidance of our experienced horsemen, including Kettley, we greenhorn mountaineers were soon riding out on patrol on relatively gentle horses. But there was one horse in our string that no one could seem to ride.

We called him "Big Red," a tall, well-muscled bay gelding with a black mane and tail. He was the biggest horse we had, almost sixteen hands high, the perfect horse for our lieutenant to ride at the head of the platoon. The trouble was, neither the lieutenant, nor any of the rest of us, so far, could handle him. So he stood tied to the picket line, while we and the lieutenant rode lesser horses.

Picket Line Duty

One Sunday, while most of the crew had weekend leave, I had picket line duty, which meant watering and graining our mounts, shoveling the manure behind them, and keeping a general eye out for their welfare. As I rested from the brutal Texas sun in the shade of a scraggly pine tree, Bill Kettley came up quietly, an unlit cigarette in his mouth as usual.

"Maybe it's time for us to try out Big Red," he mumbled through his cigarette. "Give me a hand, will you?" So I brought the big bay around into the shade, and we saddled him up, Kettley giving him a thump on his belly to be sure the cinch was tight.

For some unfathomable reason, we had been given standard western saddles, instead of the usual uncomfortable McClellan Army-issue ones. Once again checking the saddle, Kettley led the horse into a dusty clearing nearby. "Now stand clear," he said. "You know how this fellow is when he gets nervous!"

Meanwhile, the big bay stood there, every muscle aquiver, ready to explode under whoever would try to ride him. And appearing out of nowhere, but standing away a respectable distance, a dozen guys had arrived to enjoy the expected show.

But Kettley had other ideas. Talking almost inaudibly to the horse, Bill stroked his neck, patted him, and fussed with his bridle, seemingly oblivious of his audience. He was a lean little man, but hard as nails. We all expected a great exhibition of riding from him.

Kettley stuck a worn boot toe into the off stirrup, and swung up to stand in the stirrup as if to swing further into the saddle. Sweat glistening on his hide, the big horse gathered himself to buck this intruder off his back. But Kettley just stood there in the stirrup, talking softly to the bay in words none of us could hear.

Then Bill stepped down, and holding the horse's reins almost negligently, pulled a match out of his jeans and just as negligently lit up. Big Red's ears lay back, his eyes looked around wildly, but Bill didn't seem to notice. His cigarette now lit, Kettley again swung up to stand in the stirrup, again talking to the horse, and again stepping down. By this time, Big Red was shaking all over, and his sweat had turned to a light foam in the Texas heat. We in the growing audience had no idea what was happening between the little man and the big horse.

What's Going On?

Just then, a staff car drove up, and a light-colonel from headquarters climbed out. Seeing the gathering crowd, the colonel hurried over. "What's going on?" he

whispered, aware of the palpable silence of the moment.
"He's tryin' to break Big Red!" I whispered back.
"But damned if I know how!"

So we all stood, and watched, and waited. Kettley stood in the stirrup and then got down twice more. Then, so suddenly that there was an audible gasp from the crowd, Bill swung into the saddle, spurred the horse lightly, and they galloped away out of the clearing, into the long dusty road that led to the Post's main gate.

As horse and rider disappeared in the dust, we all, even the colonel, stood transfixed. One grizzled mule skinner shook his head. "I been around horses twenty years!" he said. "I ain't never seen nothin' to equal that!"

So some of us waited, and some of the crowd drifted away. The colonel got into his staff car. "Let me know what happens!" he shouted as he drove off.

It was more than an hour later when I spied the dusty figures of Kettley and Big Red trotting up the road from the gate. As if it was just another day at the ranch, Kettley dropped neatly off the big animal, his cigarette, again unlit, still in the corner of his thin mouth.

"Better water him, and clean him up a little," he said. "He worked up a good sweat out there!" Then, finally taking pity on me, he smiled his wry smile.

"Tell the lieutenant he can ride him all he wants, now. He's a good horse, just needed a stiff workout to teach him who's who!"

Sure enough, Big Red turned out to be the best horse in the outfit. The lieutenant looked like a real cavalry officer riding his big steed on parade. When we had a chance to ride him, we all agreed he was the sweetest animal we had ever handled.

Later, we learned Bill had ridden him over half of Bastrop County before bringing him home. Bill never told us what he'd talked to Big Red about. Guess that was a secret between him and the horse. But to us, Kettley and Big Red were a miracle we'd probably never see again. And this was fifty years before that book and movie about the Horse Whisperer!

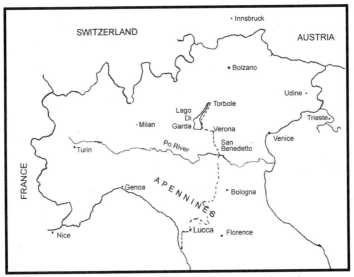

Northern Italy. The dotted line depicts the 10th Mountain
combat route from January to May, 1945.

The War Up Close

From Camp Swift, many of my buddies left; for Officer's
Candidate School, for other units, some just to get out of the
Texas heat. But in November of '44, word came that we were
finally assigned to the European Theater, to the Apennine
mountains of northern Italy. The 86th Regiment left first, then
by early January of 1945, the rest of the division was unloading off the West Point at the bombed and war-torn port of
Naples. Now we were going to see the war, up close and personal!

TWO SMOKESTACKS AND A LATEEN SAIL

We couldn't believe what was happening to us! After unit after unit of the 10th Mountain Division was loaded aboard modern U.S. Navy LCIs (Landing Craft, Infantry), it was now our turn. And the boat they had reserved for us must have been resurrected from an early 19th century shipping museum!

We had arrived in Naples aboard the West Point, previously the America, one of the biggest, fastest and most modern ships in the world. In and out of the harbor we saw dozens of modern destroyers, cruisers, LSTs and other naval craft. And now they were loading us on a rusty, weather-beaten old Italian steamer for the trip north to Livorno!

All around us were the worn, bomb-and-shell shattered buildings of Naples. The harbor was littered with the bombed-out wrecks of Italian and German ships. But none of us had expected that our golden chariot into combat was going to be the dilapidated pumpkin we saw before us on Naples' battered docks.

For three days, we had been housed in clean but war-worn apartment buildings near the harbor, waiting for the next stage in our strange journey towards combat. Some of our units had entrained for the front in the tired remnants of the Italian railroad system. Others had loaded on the gray-painted but otherwise new and clean LCI's, and were steaming north towards the division's destination near Pisa.

And now we were loading, with full combat gear and barracks bags, onto this piece of Mediterranean maritime history!

Our first clue as to the age of the vessel was its two stubby smoke stacks, already belching black smoke as its coal-fired engines built up steam for the journey. Then as we shuffled up the gang plank, and headed for our quarters, we noticed the wooden mast, jutting up forward of the ship's forecastle. A mast, on a steam vessel?

Until we were settled in our crowded troop quarters, we couldn't explore that question. But it wasn't long before we understood to what kind of transport we had been assigned.

The long, low room where our bunks were located was perhaps six feet high, with frequent overhead beams requiring even our shorter guys to stoop to move around.

The bunks were made of canvas slung between iron pipes. Each bunk was expected to hold all of our gear as well as each of us, an almost impossibly tight squeeze. When I tried out my space, I realized that, lying on my side, my hip was approximately a half inch from the bulge of the hip of the man above me.

While we were discovering all this, our ship had filled to capacity, and was getting under way. An American Navy voice came on a scratchy p.a. system.

"Now hear this! All troops fall out on deck for a body count. No exceptions!"

The Outline of Vesuvius

So we straggled up on deck, and formed up in front of our lieutenant. The buildings of Naples were already receding, and the stark outline of Vesuvius to the south reminded us where we were, and where we were going.

After the lieutenant led us through the usual ritual of hollering "Here!" when our names were called, we "fell out," and had time to look around. And there was that stubby mast looming over our heads.

One of our more nautical members explained it to us. "See the long boom, at the foot of the mast, with a rolled-up sail on top? My guess is that's a lateen sail, and its purpose is to add some wind power to this old crate when there's a following wind!"

A Lateen Sail

So he explained what a lateen sail was, and then it was time for chow. As I recall, chow was potato soup, bread, coffee and some kind of pudding for dessert. It wasn't going to be a gourmet trip, it was clear. Fortunately, we all had K-rations and some chocolate bars stuffed in our barracks bags to snack on.

I have to admit, the next hour aboard was pleasant enough. As we chugged north, black smoke billowing behind us, we watched the Italian coast to starboard fade as the sun set, then tiny lights sprang up, letting us know there were humans out there under the dark outlines of Italy's mountainous spine. We were tired enough so the announcement that the "sleeping lamp was lit" found us crawling willingly into our bunks, in spite of the crowded quarters.

One unusual fact stands out from the blur of events the next morning. After a frugal breakfast; oatmeal, bread and coffee, it was time for many of us to move our bowels. Suddenly, we realized we hadn't seen any toilets in the pissoir-like latrine!

The reason became instantly obvious. One of our sergeants had cased the situation the night before. "Follow me," was all he had to say.

Out on the starboard deck, slung over the gunwale, were two long, solid planks. Cut out at regular intervals in the wood were round holes, like those in old American privies. Beneath the planks, nothing but the streaming green and white waters of the Tyrrhenian Sea!

Needless to say, some of our number acquired instant constipation. Others braved the unsettling view of the rushing waters beneath them. In time, the plank-and-hole privy was just another experience in our new wartime world.

The weather on our second day was flawless; blue skies punctuated with fleecy white clouds and calm seas lessening the incidence of sea-sickness among the troops. Lucky for us, the U.S. Air Force had cleared the skies of enemy aircraft. In the afternoon, a warm south wind came up out of Africa, and we had our first look at our lateen sail.

Now it was the turn of the Italian crew to function without the U.S. Navy seamen. Untying the cords lashing the sail, they hauled the boom up to perhaps a twenty degree angle, then swung it out over the rushing water. Next they unfurled the sail, attached through ropes and pulleys to the top of the mast. Once unfurled and stretched tight, the big, faded-red triangular sail caught the following south wind, and billowed out to starboard. Even the landlubbers among us could feel the old coal-burning craft pick up speed, pushed along by a friendly wind from Africa.

The Green Hills of Italy

The rest of our journey was pretty much the same. Plain food, crowded quarters, the daily adventure on the plank-and-hole privy. Always to the east, the rolling green hills of Italy, with occasional small stone villages, bridges and glimpses of narrow highways and the thin dark line of a railway.

The calm seas and south winds persisted, so we were told the old freighter was going to break its own record - Naples to Livorno - with the help of the lateen sail. Our arrival at this northern port, swarming with jeeps and trucks and armed soldiers, brought us back with a rush to the realization that we were going to war.

But our days on the rusty old steamship could have been a lot worse. We learned a lot about coal-fired boilers and lateen sails and plank privies. It was an appropriate introduction to battered old Europe, where we were about to fight in a modern war.

One of the mountain villages, San Marcello, where we were
introduced to wartime Italy, the Apennines on the skyline.

DEJA VU NEAR BAGNI DI LUCCA

After tent camping for a day or two in Pisa's Kings
Park, following our steamer voyage up from Naples, we
of the 87th Recon threw our gear in some six-by-sixes
provided by Service Company, and moved to Bagni di
Lucca, a few miles north of Lucca proper. Here we were
housed in an Italian villa, whose owners, we assumed,
had been dispossessed because of Fascist connections.
In fact, the paintings and photos still on the walls
included many poses of affluent Italians smiling alongside their now dishonored Duce.

Our assignment, the lieutenant told us, was to patrol
into the Apennine foothills, partly as our first combat
reconnaissance practice, and partly to seek out the limits of German positions. Our orders were not to fire
unless fired upon, so as to camouflage as much as possible our own troop movements and dispositions.

Anxious to appear as soldierly as possible, the lieutenant gathered some of us in the villa library, and spread a Royal Italian Auto Club map on a table. The map, (our military maps not yet being available,) described our location, and the immediate mountain foothills north of Lucca.

"Our first mission," the lieutenant said, pointing to a dot on the map, "is to reconnoiter this mountain village, to ascertain if it is still in enemy hands."

We all moved close around, and stared at the dot denoting the village, its name inscribed in tiny type above the strange hachures, typical of European maps, denoting the mountain terrain. For some reason still a mystery to me, I was the first to speak.

"At least there's no more Germans in the village," I said.

"And how the hell do you know that?" said Loren, our Intelligence Sergeant. "Smart you may be, but I don't remember you've ever been clairvoyant!"

Embarrassed, I looked around at my fellow Recon types for a sympathetic eye. But they all were staring at me, including the now impatient lieutenant.

Tell Us More

"If you know so much," he smiled, "tell us more! Tell us how to get there, and what we'll find when we do!"

Now surrounded by cynically unbelieving soldiers, I somehow found a surety that hadn't been there moments before. I held up both hands to silence the amused mutterings that erupted around me.

"Look," I began. "I don't know how I know, but it's as if I had been in that village before. I can tell you about it, if you'll let me."

While most of the soldiers around me hooted their disbelief, I could see that Loren was at least willing to listen. "Give Parker a chance," he said." If he's wrong, we'll soon find out!"

Though I could find it again on an Italian map, I can't for the life of me remember the tiny village's name. But somewhat encouraged by Loren's remark, I asked for a sheet of blank paper, and started to draw.

"It's a walled town, built on a narrow ridge." I began. "Probably built in the Middle Ages. There are only two gates in the walls, a small one in the south wall, and the main entrance gate to the north."

As I clumsily drew rough outlines of the walls, my companions quieted down, and seemed at least momentarily to want to listen.

"There are only two routes to the village," I went on. "One, just a mule trail, leads to the narrow south gate. The other, big enough at least for a jeep, and maybe a six-by, loops around the ridge to the north and enters the main gate."

Here I stopped, thinking I'd said enough. But the lieutenant, convinced I was somehow conning him and the others, urged me to continue.

"OK," I muttered. "Here's what I think I know about the place. In the center of the village is a cobblestone-paved square. On the west end, a big building, probably the city hall. On the other end, a stone church with a square tower."

"Is that all?" laughed the lieutenant. "No other details?"

I blushed, uncertain if I should continue. "One other thing," I mumbled. "There's a fountain, and a watering trough, in the middle of the square!"

With that the others all laughed, and urged me on. "More, more!" they hollered. But the lieutenant had heard enough.

"All right," he said. "Tomorrow, Parker will lead a patrol up the trail to the south gate. If there is one!" he added. "He'll take a radio. The rest of us go by jeep on the road to the north. Once he's in the village, Parker will radio us. We'll see if he knows what he's talking about!"

The Trail Up Mount Marcy

That night, I scarcely slept, wondering over and over again where this mysterious information had come from. True, I had had one similar experience as a teenager. When our climbing group lost the trail near the summit of Mount Marcy in northern New York, I described the route and led the group by a circuitous track right to the above-timberline top of the mountain. But I never knew *how I knew* the proper way through a maze of trees and rocks to the summit!

Next day was "fish or cut bait" for me and my patrol of six. Driven close by truck, we found the narrow trail, and started up without difficulty. Not knowing what to expect, we were in combat formation, with guns loaded and ready. Above us, we could see a small gate apparently piercing the village's south wall.

Just then, out of this gate appeared a man in rough clothes leading a small Italian mule. He soon spied us climbing towards him, and stopped to wait for us.

"Buon giorno," I began. " Noi siamo Americani - soldati!" This was about the limit of my Italian language capabilities.

"Yes, yes," he said, in almost accentless American English. "I know who you are! Buon giorno to you, too. Lucky for you, the Germans have been gone from here for days!"

Feeling a lot easier, I told him what we were assigned to do, without revealing my efforts at clairvoyance.

"Tell you what," our newfound friend continued. "I'll tie up mulo here, and take you up to the village!" In short order, we found ourselves guided up the trail, with our friend Joe (Guiseppi, he admitted) rattling on about his twenty years of work in the Pittsburg steel mills.

He ushered us through the gate, which seemed scarcely wide enough for his mule, and into the village square. To the amazement of all of us, it was just as I had described it, but with the north and south walls lined with houses and shops. Most importantly, the opposite gate was broad enough for either jeeps or trucks!

I unslung my big walkie-talkie, and keyed in the lieutenant."Come on up the road and into town, the north gate is plenty wide! And there's no Germans!"

A Guided Tour

Soon the little square seemed full of GIs, trying out their Italian and sharing cigarettes and chocolate with a rapidly swelling crowd of local citizens. Joe promptly attached himself to the lieutenant, so I followed as he conducted a guided tour of the village.

"This is the mayor's office," he said proudly, pointing out the large building to the west. "That's our chiesa, our church. Built around ten hundred, that's why there's no tall steeple."

"This fontana has the finest water around! Help yourself - fill your canteens!"

As Joe chattered on, I saw the lieutenant sneaking looks at me. He, as well as all the other Americans, could see I had been right about all the main details of the village.

Years later, hearing this story, my spiritually inclined friends assumed that, in another life, I had lived in that northern Italian region, even though, in studying my family heritage, I can find no marriages between New England Yankees and Italians.

Strangely, the lieutenant never again queried me about my detailed knowledge of that ancient Italian village. And I never had another attack of the clairvoyance that visited me in Bagni di Lucca, and on top of Mount Marcy. Maybe twice in a lifetime was enough!

Vidiciatico, where we were headquarted while we patrolled the front. The church steeple roof was shattered by German shells.

BETRAYED BY A SNEEZE!

In a way, we in the Regimental Reconnaissance Platoon were lucky. Most of the men in the line companies got a sudden and brutal introduction to combat during their first day or night confrontation with the enemy. In our case, we conducted night patrols, manned observation posts, interrogated prisoners, and otherwise got some exposure to danger, and to the enemy, before being thrust into a direct combat situation.

Our first brush with the Germans and their accurate artillery happened shortly after we moved into some ancient stone houses and barns in the still-medieval town of Vidiciatico, on a north slope facing the twin massifs of Riva Ridge and Mount Belvedere. Our lieutenant immediately spotted the 11th century stone church steeple in the middle of town, thought it made a perfect location for an observation post, and assigned several of us to man an op in the north-facing embrasure in the tower's belfry.

Apparently one of us was careless about visible movement, or the glint of light on our binoculars, because in no time German shells zeroed in on the tower, destroyed its slate and wooden roof, and drove us to shelter down the rickety wooden stairs. Our regimental commander, Colonel Fowler, chewed out the lieutenant for unnecessarily endangering an historic structure, and ordered us to find another op. It was our first convincing exposure to German artillery fire, directed precisely by their observers atop Riva Ridge, our division's first battle objective!

Though not nearly as effective as the church tower, our future op's in old barns, houses and on mountain ridges at least allowed us to keep track of any major movements of the enemy. But Colonel Fowler wanted more immediate intelligence. So our next assignment was night patrols; probing the locations of enemy lines.

I remember well our first patrol. Dressed warmly in layers of wool, shoe packs on our feet and white camouflage suits over all, we passed our own lines just after dark and suddenly were in no-man's-land. Here the frozen snow-covered terrain fell steeply beneath our feet, each step requiring a careful balancing act as we dropped into gullies, then climbed each opposite slope in the dark.

The man on point stopped frequently, feeling in front of himself with a stripped tree branch for trip wires or other obstacles, straining his ears for any suspicious sound. At first, dealing with the steep and broken terrain kept us warm. But during the many stops, the freezing night air began to seep into our clothing, making us wonder how long we could endure this exposure.

Then we began to climb, and the unmistakable dark profile of the enemy-occupied ridge loomed over us. As we waited for our lieutenant to choose our next move, one of the guys, after an heroic effort to suppress it, exploded in a loud sneeze.

All Hell Broke Loose

In an instant, it seemed that all hell had broken loose. A machine gun on the ridge, firing frequently spaced incendiaries, raked the slope where we lay. Enemy guard dogs began barking. Then we heard the telltale "pop" of a flare opening over our heads.

Suddenly our nighttime world was as bright as day. The German flare, swaying under its parachute, seemed to take forever to descend. Meanwhile, flattened into the snow, we lay motionless, our white camouflage, we hoped, effectively hiding us from the Germans.

When the flare extinguished, and the machine gun fell silent, we lay for what seemed forever, beneath the enemy position. Apparently the Germans, unable to see any large body of American troops in the winter darkness, had decided we were not a threat worth expending ammunition over.

Cautiously, the lieutenant crawled back among his men, whispering that we were through for the night. First crawling down hill, then stumbling back up the mountain behind a new point man, we returned to our own lines.

Here in the darkness we encountered a potentially dangerous moment. It was now past midnight, and the day's password had expired, and a new one was called for. Our point man, not remembering the new password, but cleverer than most, said aloud, "I don't know the new password, but I bet the Krauts never heard of Red Cliff, Colorado!"

Hearing the name of the tiny town nearest to our training grounds at Camp Hale, in inimitable American accents, the guards behind our barricades chuckled, and hollered "Pass, patrol! But next time, you might not be so lucky!"

Back at regimental headquarters, our lieutenant identified the exact location of the German positions on a map, somewhere near Rocca Corneta, while the rest of us sacked out in a ramshackle hay barn. It was the first of many patrols, but none was ever burned so clearly on my memory as the night when we were almost betrayed by a sneeze.

American artillery at Corona, on Belvedere's west ridge, answering a German barrage. The northern end of Riva Ridge outlined beyond.

FIRST COMBAT ON BELVEDERE

The night after the 86th regiment's spectacular success on Riva Ridge on February 18th, we of the 87th and 85th regiments were committed to a second night attack, this one on Mount Belvedere on the 19th. Because I had led night patrols in the neighborhood of Corona, I was assigned as first scout for the First Battalion, 87th, whose planned route led by Corona village on the Belvedere west ridge. It would be my initial combat experience, and night combat at that!

I remember waiting, hidden by the ancient stone buildings of Querciola, our new regimental headquarters, until night fell, then moving out ahead of B Company, at first over frozen snow. It was almost exactly my route of several nights before. That night, directly under the dark outlines of the Corona buildings, I had nearly triggered a "bouncing betty" mine, which would have ended my scouting career then and there. But on February 19th, our route over frozen snow relieved my concern about German "schuh" mines. We soon had a lot more than mines to worry about.

Suddenly, the muted sound of our shoepacks crunching the hard snow was drowned by the staccato sound of German machine and burp guns, and the blackness was torn by German tracers, searching the slopes where we stood. Everyone flattened himself in the snow, staring up at the ridge where the guns continued to blaze. A small tree just in front of me was cut in two by a bullet, and plopped onto my helmet. It was time to find shelter.

Ahead and to the left I could barely sense a small ravine, On my stomach, I crawled into its shelter, and found a lieutenant and several B Company soldiers huddling below the German line of fire. None of us had fired yet - our orders were "bayonets, not bullets" until we closed with the enemy.

They Can't Reach Us

Over the noise of gunfire, I hollered to the lieutenant. "They can't reach us under the terrace wall, except with grenades. Let's crawl ahead, then move up slope to the right." One by one we first crawled, then crouching climbed the slope, with German fire still streaking the night sky overhead. As we filed out of a gully into open fields, the fire from the German positions at Corona lessened, but more mortar and machine gun fire descended upon us from higher on the ridge as we joined the rest of the company, and swung east up Belvedere proper.

The rest of that night remains a blur of cold, gunfire, mortar shells, German grenades and huddling behind any kind of cover as we advanced, paused, took cover, then advanced again. As we climbed, I occasionally heard strangled cries and sensed, rather than saw, men falling beside me. I was no longer a scout, but just part of a long line of advancing dark shapes, itching to fire our weapons but ordered not to.

For what seemed like an hour, we had to halt, while

The battle order for our first few days of combat.
Riva Ridge, left and Monte Belvedere, center

other units moved up beside our scattered formation. Then we moved out again, always stumbling in the dark, always climbing, firing now at phantom shapes ahead, struggling with the barbed wire the Germans had strung to slow us down. Suddenly, as the skies lightened to the east, we found ourselves on the flattened summit ridge of the mountain. The Germans, for the moment at least, had been driven back. B Company men began digging in on the ridge's north slope, and I looked for and found an officer among the still indistinct torn and muddy uniforms.

"Sir," I began, but he raised a tired hand and grinned through the pall of dirt on his face. "I know, you have to return to headquarters. Just tell them, B Company has reached its objective. It's too soon to report on casualties, and Kraut positions. You'd better get out of here, they're sure to counter attack soon!"

He turned back to his men, and I started down the mountain. I still had my carbine, but somewhere in the night I had lost my helmet. Just before the summit, I had given a medic my mountain jacket, to cover a wounded line company man. So as I half ran down the mountain, my uniform was a shirt and sweater, mountain pants, and the Navy watch cap I'd worn under my helmet against the winter cold. As it turned out, not the right clothing to identify me, in the dawn light, as an American soldier.

And the lieutenant had been right, there would be a counter attack. Three quarters of my way down the shoulder of Belvedere, German artillery opened up from the dark valley to the north. Clearly intended to stop the progress of troops coming up to reinforce our first wave, the barrage caught me turning south into the open fields above Corona. As round after round of 105 shells exploded around me, I had no choice but to flatten myself in the dirt, get up, run a yard or so, then flatten myself again. The frozen dirt of the fields soon caked my clothes, face and hands, even my carbine with instant mud.

One Last 105

As I lay in a shell hole, trying to summon the will to move on, one last 105 shell screamed in and exploded three or four feet to my left. The barrage was over, but instead of the blessed silence I expected, my head rang with the explosion, and echoed with a shrill buzzing that has persisted, though not as loudly, to this day.

Somehow, I picked myself out of the shell hole, and moved on. All that existed in my mind was getting to headquarters, and reporting what I knew. But my introduction to warfare wasn't quite over.

As I stumbled down the sloping field into the woods below, a group of GI's came out of the woods in combat formation, the point man carrying an ugly looking BAR. He, and every man in the lead squad swung their guns up, and someone hollered "Halt!"

I suddenly knew how I must have looked to these men, themselves on the way up the mountain to join in the battle. I dropped my carbine, and raised my arms. More frightened than I'd been all night, I was about to say "I'm American!", knowing every one of them wanted to kill me, sure that I was a German. Then a voice from the squad's rear hollered "It's OK - I know him!"

The Voice That Saved Me

One by one, the men lowered their guns, and the voice that had saved me materialized into my friend Sammy, now a PFC with L Company. "Where the hell you been?" he demanded, and when I managed to croak "On top of Belvedere", he shrugged, and motioned me on. The unit parted to let me through, then continued on their way into combat. I learned later that L Company and one other would have, over the next two and a half months, the highest combat casualties in the 87th.

After reporting to headquarters in Querciola, I submitted to a cursory physical from our regimental surgeon, then hitched a ride in a six-by-six back to Vidiciatico. As I watched the long lines of GI's plodding up the road towards our front lines, I thanked my lucky stars I was in Recon, where I would only periodically be exposed to the worst of this war, the kind of danger they would experience almost every day they were in combat.

Years later, I learned from Sammy how he knew it was me, there on the shoulder of Mount Belvedere. "Other people must have told you this before," he began. "Nobody, I mean nobody, has a walk like yours. Like a New England farmer, stumbling behind a plow!" Not very flattering, but just enough to save my life, that morning of February 20th, 1945.

THE FIRST SERGEANT'S KP CALL

This potentially serious confrontation began because we Recon platoon guys had been excused from KP and other menial company duties. Sounds discriminatory, but the reason was the hard fact that we were out on night patrol or on op duty every night, and needed sleep during the day to stay alive.

So we were sound asleep in an old hay barn when the barn door was kicked open, and our heavy-set first sergeant, his pistol, a menacing .357, slung low beneath his fat gut, stood outlined in brilliant sunlight in the doorway. As luck would have it, the first sleeper on the hay-covered floor was Nap, who sat up, blinking in the harsh light. The sergeant strode over, and kicked Nap's sleeping bag.

"OK, Nap," he growled. "You're first. You're on KP, starting now!"

Out of the barn's shadows, a quiet voice spoke. "Sergeant, you know damn well we're excused from company duty!" It was Loren, our always reasonable intelligence sergeant.

"I don't give a shit if you're excused!" the sergeant grunted. "I need guys for KP, and you guys are elected!"

The rest of us, partially hidden in the shadows, had meanwhile been watching Nap. I should explain that, in addition to being a brilliant skier and climber, he was half Ojibway Indian, and a magnificent physical specimen.

Dressed only in GI shorts, Nap slid out of his sleeping bag, stood up, and stretched, the muscles under his dark skin rippling. Quietly, he walked over to the barn wall, picked up his carbine, and jacked a round into the chamber.

In two quick strides, Nap confronted the sergeant, thrusting the muzzle of his carbine into the man's ample belly. "Sergeant," he said, using the man's last name. "I want you to turn around, walk to the company office (a room in a nearby stone farmhouse), and tell the Captain you want to transfer out!"

The first sergeant mumbled something, spun around, and half ran toward the farmhouse, apparently forgetting he was armed with that ugly .357 pistol. As he hurried away, Nap hollered after him. "If we ever see you again, I'll be the first one to put a bullet in that fat belly!"

We later learned the captain signed the first sergeant's transfer papers without even asking a question. Soon, we had a new first sergeant, a guy we grew to respect and admire. But we never saw the old sergeant again. And we never pulled company duty, including KP, until after the end of the war.

The landscape near La Serra, on the little mountain known as Punchboard Hill.

PUNCHBOARD HILL

The Germans were always punctual. Precisely at 5:15, shells came screaming over the mountain above us, and exploded around us in the terrible, haphazard pattern we had come to dread. Each in his own foxhole, the men of the Recon op squad hunkered down and waited, afraid, for the evening barrage to end.

We were on the American side of a little mountain the Italians called La Serra, but we called Punchboard Hill, where the Third Battalion had been dug in for days. The chestnut forest that had covered the hill was already decimated by a constant rain of German shells. Only a few ten to twenty foot-high tree trunks still stood above the brutal tangle of broken limbs, shell holes and shards of wood that mantled the hillside. More than 1000 shells a day had exploded on the battalion, and their casualties had been heavy.

Beneath the tangle of broken trees, the men of the Third were living like embattled moles, dug deep in the forest soil, their foxholes and dugouts roofed with trunks and limbs torn off by the shelling.

Punchboard was one of two small mountains that guarded a pass through this part of the Apennine chain. Our General George Hays wanted access to the road that ran through the pass, so our division could advance.The Germans were desperate to stop him. Division headquarters had ordered my outfit to establish an observation post on the top of the hill to monitor what the Germans were up to before the regiment launched the expected attack

We had arrived in mid-day, normally a quiet time for German artillery. There was no room in the chestnut woods for us to dig in, so we dumped our gear in a steep clearing just east of the woods, and Hawk and I crawled up to the ridge line to find a place for our observation post.

We located a shattered tree in a small depression on the ridge that looked promising, and slid back down to describe it to the lieutenant.

"Sounds good," he said. "We'll wait 'til dark to set up. Meanwhile, you guys better dig in - the Krauts always shell at supper time."

A Lousy Place For Foxholes

Our rocky clearing was a lousy place for foxholes - mostly shallow soil, shale and hardpan. But I found a little bench where water had collected and soft soil built up. I began to dig.

One thing we had learned in two months of combat was the trajectories of German artillery. The 88's and 40-mm ack-acks had flat trajectories; the rockets, and the shells of 105's and mortars, better suited to mountain warfare, arced high over a mountain, then fell in a slanting dive, hitting the first projection they came to on the other side - a tree, a house, a man. As I dug my foxhole, I began to realize my little bench could be a perfect target for a high-angle 105!

I dropped my shovel and looked around. The others were busy scratching out shallow foxholes farther up the slope. I looked down. I had already dug a deep hole in the soft earth, with room for another alongside. Despite the exposure, it looked comfortable and safe, and it was with a faint sense of doing something wrong that I picked up shovel and pack, moved up the slope, and started another hole in the tough shale.

It was about four o'clock when Loren and Johnny arrived from headquarters, little more than an hour before the daily Krupp Express roared through. Loren, our Intelligence Sergeant and the brains of our outfit, dropped his pack and hurried up to report to the lieutenant. Johnny looked at my abandoned hole, scratched his head under his helmet, and hollered, "Whose hole?"

I was sitting on the edge of my new foxhole, eating a K-ration." I dug it," I answered. "But I don't like the location! Sticks out of the slope too much!"

Returning, Loren surveyed the situation, and settled it. "Looks OK to me - we don't have much time! Johnny, you dig in next to me here, I'll take Parker's hole."

So Johnny dug quickly, while the rest of us ate, or cleaned our weapons, or thought about home. Loren settled in my hole and in the dim light went to work on his daily intelligence summary.

It was nearly dark when the lieutenant's voice drifted down to us. "Everybody dug in?" A muted chorus answered - "Yep, OK, Si, Tenente (that was Wop), Friggin' A, Yes, Mother! (that was Bird Dog). The silence that followed was immediately shattered by the first German shell - the barrage was on schedule.

We Cowered In Our Holes

So we cowered in our holes, and our world was reduced to darkness, the scream of shells, ear-splitting explosions and the incessant shuddering of the ground beneath us. Later, we agreed that night's bombardment seemed to have been meant specifically for our op

119

squad. Clearly, the Krauts didn't want the 10th Mountain Division breaking through that pass!

At last, the shelling stopped. Again, the lieutenant's voice floated down. "Report in, guys, that was a nasty one!" One by one, our voices came out of the dark. There was no answer from Loren and Johnny.

"Parker, you're closest," the lieutenant called, his voice strained and anxious. "Check 'em out!" I crawled out of the foxhole, and groped in the dark down to the bench below. The acrid smell of cordite, burned soil and flesh hit me with a wave of nausea. I knew what I'd find.

"Parker, what happened?" The lieutenant now sounded close to panic. Swallowing my horror, I croaked a reply - "They're gone, sir. Direct hit!"

I must have fainted, then, or blacked out somehow. I awoke to the muted voices of the lieutenant and sergeant, flashlights flickering, and shadowy men working around Loren and Johnny's foxholes. I helped to close the body bags, and carried a corner of one of them almost a mile to the nearest road.

Our sober procession, lit only by flashlights and the red glow of cigarettes, ended by the Malandrone Bridge. We loaded the bags on a medic's jeep and watched it bump away over the shell-torn road.

The lieutenant gathered us around him. "No op duty tonight. By radio, Col. Fowler has relieved us for a few days. A truck's on the way to take us back to headquarters."

I sat on the road bank, lit a cigarette, and stared blankly into the lightening sky to the east. I didn't know it then, but that blankness would cloud my mind for days. Finally, a week later, the shock of that night on Punchboard Hill gave way to a stronger instinct. Somehow, I had to shed the awful past, and try to live out the rest of the war.

The intensity of the early March advance is illustrated by the ruins of Castel d'Aiano, shelled by both sides.

The Last Range

As a division, we had proven ourselves in combat with the sensational capture of Riva Ridge, Belvedere and Della Torraccia. General Hays felt we had the Germans on the run. Fifth Army headquarters, who were used to slow, massive movements of troops and supplies, thought we should wait for the Army to catch up. But there was one more breakthrough to accomplish before Hays would stop - the last range of hills after the key city of Castel d'Aiano. Then, it was said, we could rest until the spring offensive in mid-April.

THE DENTIST IN THE APPLE ORCHARD

One of the benefits of the modern army, which I suddenly had to call on, was dentistry in the combat zone. During the few quiet days between offensives, when we were manning an observation post on Mount Della Vedetta, my jaw began to ache so urgently that I went on sick call, and requested some emergency dentistry, if it was possible in that time and place.

The very next day, our company clerk called on our op telephone, and told me to report to regimental headquarters at 16:00 hours Friday, to have my tooth fixed.

"Regimental headquarters!" I said, "There's no clinic at regimental headquarters!"

"He brings his own clinic," the clerk said. "Report Friday on time, or your jaw will go on hurting! There's only one dentist for the whole damn outfit - he's outta' here Saturday!"

So I chewed on some cloves I got from the mess sergeant, slept very little and reported about three o'clock Friday to headquarters, which was a dilapidated old stone farmhouse tucked among apple and cherry trees a half mile from the nearly ruined town of Pietra Colora.

The clinic the dentist brought with him, it turned out, was a metal dental chair, with an attached swinging tray, a foot pump to operate his drill, and an ancient wooden chair from the farmhouse to hold his leather case full of instruments. A metal dish, containing what was apparently alcohol to sterilize his tools, also sat precariously on the chair.

All of this was set up on an irregular slope under a

blossoming apple tree. I watched, fearfully, while the lieutenant/dentist pumped and drilled and pried on the teeth of the men who had been lined up ahead of me. The final step of this procedure, when the dentist was through, was to have each man rinse his bloody mouth with water from an army canteen!

Finally it was my turn - I was the last of the dental officer's half-dozen patients, and it was late - almost five in the afternoon. I knew, though the dentist didn't, that the usual German bombardment was likely to start around five, or 17:00 hours that evening. And right on schedule, German shells began coming in over our heads just as the dentist said "Next!"

Immediate Alarm

The dentist's immediate alarm was almost funny. As I settled uneasily in his chair, he dropped his tools on the tray and scuttled for the old farmhouse. A few Kraut shells screamed overhead, and exploded in the fields below. Then there was a lull in the shelling.

Looking a little shamefaced, the dentist finally appeared in the farmhouse doorway, then briskly introduced himself, examined my jaw, and began pumping with his foot and drilling into the offending filling. No painkilling shot or drug - this was field dentistry at its most basic.

Beneath the filling, the tooth was seriously decayed. The drilling continued, until a gaping cavity, every millimeter of it painful, had been cleared out. Just as the lieutenant was assuring me that he had "Got it all!" the shelling began again. And, again, my dental torturer/savior disappeared in a flash into the cellar of the headquarters building.

As I sat there, at once in great pain and highly amused, I wondered if I should tell him the truth about my apparent bravery under fire. We all knew that Mount Della Vedetta, looming above headquarters, was high enough so no German shells, though a nuisance, had steep enough trajectories to reach our location in the apple orchard.

In a few minutes, the dentist appeared, this time full of questions. "How come," he began, "You can sit here, apparently unconcerned, when the damn shells are screaming over our heads?"

I was sorely tempted to tell him how "us veterans" were so inured to shelling that we couldn't bother to take cover. But since my jaw was still sore, and the cavity still open, I figured he had to get back to work. So I told him about the fortuitous shelter the mountain provided us, and he resumed his bloody business in my jaw. The Krauts shelled us twice more, but the lieutenant, like the veteran he now was, never flinched as the shells whistled overhead while he proceeded with the delicate stuffing of my cavity.

When he was through, I had rinsed out my mouth, and had a filling that would last for several years, I apologized for fooling him during the first two bombardments.

"That's OK," he grinned. "I learned a valuable lesson. And, I have a great story to tell when I get home!" Then he shook my hand, and added, "Part of my story will be about the corporal who sat in the apple orchard, with a seriously sore jaw, and never complained once about the lieutenant who abandoned him every time some German shells came over!"

The towers of Florence seen from across the Arno River.

Final Offensive

We did rest in late March and early April. We took baths at Montecatini, watched opera in Florence, patroled and manned op's, with little danger from a temporarily beaten but rapidly reorganizing German army. Then, the day after we had sadly learned of President Roosevelt's passing, we launched, on April 14th, our final offensive of the war.

THE ROAD BACK

We were part of a narrow, winding caravan of men and vehicles headed for the Po Valley. Smoke hung like a sooty pall over everything, smoke, and the nauseous smell of burned farmhouses; wood, straw, plaster, manure and the incinerated bodies of animals and men.

Occasionally, the freight-train rumble of a giant German shell would disturb the air overhead and eventually explode somewhere in the rear. The sergeant said there was a railroad gun down in the Po Valley, fourteen inches or so. The Krauts must have been desperate to stop our advance, using a weapon like that.

And just in front of us, and on both flanks, the fighting and killing went on. As usual, the line companies were taking a beating. We were just part of the regimental column, waiting for our turn to play a part in the war.

It was clearly hard going for the rifle companies. We could see white bursts of cannon fire along the ridges ahead, and frequent errant 88 or 105 shells would scream in and explode near us, sending all of us, including the officers, diving for the ditches. When asked when, or if, we'd get to fight, the lieutenant would shrug and say "Soon enough. We'll be in the Po Valley soon enough."

But the killing went on, and the road leading back with just room enough for stretcher bearers, prisoners and an occasional jeep, was crowded with the tattered remnants of two armies. Sometimes, two or four GIs would be carrying a wounded German on a stretcher. Then two Germans, guarded by a bandaged GI with a rifle, carrying a wounded American.

Two American stretcher bearers trudged into view, themselves bloodied, carrying a bloodier American officer on a stretcher. The lead bearer was an old friend.

"Sully!" I blurted, but he shook his head, his eyes fixed on the rough track. "See you later." His voice was hoarse and barely audible. "See you later, if there is a later." Then they were gone.

With the column stalled, we sat on ditch banks, and waited, listening to the grim sounds of combat ahead. A medic sergeant with a jeep bumped towards us on a narrow country road that connected to our larger one. Seeing the lieutenant, he stopped, and leaned wearily on the steering wheel.

"I need some help, sir" he said. "If you don't mind, half a dozen men, for maybe a half hour?"

The lieutenant pointed at the nearest six of us, then climbed in the jeep. "Follow along," he said. "It's the least we can do."

Wheeling the jeep around on our wider road, the medic drove back the way he'd come, we six following on foot. As we neared a shattered Italian village, I began to guess why we were there. That sick smell of burned buildings hovered over everything.

10th Mountain stretcher bearers returning from combat

Body Bags

Stopping just short of the village, the medic climbed out, looked wearily at us, then pointed at an empty six-by-six parked with its tail gate pointing into the village. "The body bags are in the truck," the medic said. "I suggest you form three teams of two. German bodies first, then Americans. We gotta get 'em out'a here fast, they don't last long in this weather. Get names from the Americans - I gotta record 'em. The Krauts can wait."

So we began the awful task of sliding the bodies of the Germans and Americans that were sprawled in and around the village into the cotton mattress covers, first reading the Americans' dog tags. It must have been an horrific battle, for some of the GI's and Germans had fallen close to one another. Many were mangled by artillery, or rocket explosions. Others had taken single projectiles in the chest or head.

While we hesitantly ripped open shirts, and read the dog-tags out loud, the medic, seated in the jeep with a clip-board and official forms, penciled the names on a form. It had been a Second Battalion company involved in taking this unnamed hamlet. I had known several of the guys now officially on the list of KIA's.

With all of the silent bags laid out around the truck, we began lifting them, Germans first, then Americans, into the six-by-six. At this point, the lieutenant and the driver of the truck lent welcome hands. The larger bodies weren't easy, and as they piled up, two of us had to climb up, and stack the still forms, like cordwood, forward in the truck body. I never asked how many dead men we handled that day - I didn't want to know.

Bloodied Hands

Finally, it was over - more like an hour and a half than the half hour the medic had promised. We washed our bloodied hands at the barn-yard well, then, leaving the medic and the truck driver with their gruesome charges, we hiked silently back to the column, just in time to hear orders echoing down the road. "Move 'em out, move 'em out!"

We never saw the truck, or the driver, or the medic again. We later learned they tried to move such vehicles at night, so rear echelon troops would be spared the sight of their cargoes.

And the lieutenant was right. For the next two weeks, after we reached the flat fields of the Po Valley, our outfit had its share of the war. Years later in Austria, I passed a burning farm building. The acrid smoke from straw, plaster, wood and manure was all that was needed to revive the memory of a terrible afternoon. That narrow Italian track had been, for too many young soldiers on both sides, the final road back.

SPY HUNT

We should have expected something like it, I guess. The German Army was breaking up all around us. The action was fluid - enemy troops fighting in front of us, while all along our columns other Germans under guard trudged wearily back toward the temporary Prisoner-Of-War stockades, built hurriedly to contain a beaten foe. And loose in the countryside, other Germans, switching from uniforms to rough farm clothes, trying desperately to avoid capture because they'd been told we would torture, then kill them, POW's or not.

So we should have suspected that some of our own rear-echelon warriors, who had scarcely heard a shot fired in anger, would take this chance to round up fleeing Germans in civilian clothes, and kill them as spies, as their contribution to the war they had never experienced first hand. But we never dreamed such a thing would happen in our midst.

The day before the 10th Mountain Division moved into the Po Valley, after nearly four months in the mountains, was preparation for more combat for those of us in the Recon platoon. When we returned to regimental headquarters, an ancient farmer's villa, for reports and briefings, an ugly rumor awaited us. One of our guys, assigned to headquarters because of illness, had heard the company commander and company clerk bragging about their first expedition, hunting for "spies."

None of us would have had the slightest compunction about capturing, or even killing, real spies caught in a combat situation. But these two, apparently, were simply looking for Germans in civilian clothes, and plain soldiers or real spies, would shoot them, and feel like heroes to themselves and their own kind.

We were talking about all this when our platoon sergeant spoke up. "How many of you approve of what the captain is doing?" he asked quietly.

We looked around. No one spoke, though several shook their heads. The sergeant continued. "What he's trying to do may be legally correct, according to the Geneva Convention. But do any of you think it's right?"

Again there was silence, and a slow shaking of heads. Each of us was waiting for another to speak first. Finally Henderson got up in his leisurely way, but his voice was strained, his manner vehement. "It's fuckin' criminal, is what it is. They've gotta be stopped." A buzz of angry talk from everyone confirmed his comment.

A Warning Hand

The sergeant held up a warning hand. "Henderson's right. But so far they've done nothing but talk. Let's watch, and wait - maybe nothin' will come of it."

So we went to supper, the first hot chow we'd had in weeks, then collapsed in a hay barn for some much needed sleep. Next day, the incident all but forgotten, we spread out on a variety of tasks; guarding a bridge, scouting for flanking roads, carrying messages to other units. Tomorrow was jumping off day for the division's dash to the Po River, so everything had to be wrapped up tight before morning.

At supper, we knew immediately something was wrong. Our platoon sergeant wore a pained scowl, the lieutenant looked furtive, and worried sick. As we washed our mess kits, the sergeant whispered "Meet in the barn," then disappeared.

Someone had a stubby candle stuck in a beer bottle, burning on top of a wheelbarrow. Otherwise, the barn was wrapped in gloom. No one was surprised when the sergeant hurried in, and in a hoarse voice confirmed our fears.

"They've fuckin' done it," he rasped. "They rounded up two Germans, brought 'em here, and killed 'em both - shot 'em against the wall in the courtyard And they're braggin' about it, to anyone who'll listen!"

The silence in the barn was almost palpable when, again, it was Henderson who spoke. "So tell us, sergeanto, what do we do now?"

The sergeant hesitated a long moment before replying. "As you've already guessed, the lieutenant will do nothing - it's the old officers' code. If anything's gonna be done, it'll have to be us that does it. Apparently there's nobody in the rest of the company that cares about this like we do."

The silence that greeted his words was, if anything, deeper than before. Then, as a group, we began quietly to discuss what each of us had, almost to a man, decided what it was that needed to be done.

Finally, the sergeant summarized for all of us, then concluded. "We need to decide time, and place. And I need two volunteers to go with me."

Somehow it worked out that we'd visit the captain in the morning, just after chow - the sergeant, Henderson and me. Then we all rolled into our sleeping bags or blankets. I never knew about the others, but I was still wide awake when the farmer's old rooster announced the dawn, from the courtyard where the two Germans still lay in the dust.

A Cup of Weak Coffee

Wishing for a stiff brandy, or a glass of wine, I settled for a canteen cup of weak coffee for breakfast, tried to spruce up my uniform a bit, and checked that my carbine was cleaned and loaded. Then I met Henderson and the sergeant outside the door to the captain's temporary office. The sergeant's .45 hung at his belt, and Henderson, like me, carried his carbine.

The sergeant looked and sounded grim. "Let me do

the talking," he whispered. "You guys are witnesses - this may not end here." Then he knocked, and the captain gruffly said "Come in."

Seated behind the farmer's rough-hewn work table, the captain was his usual small but natty self. I had never seen him in anything but a spotless uniform. "What can I do for you gentlemen." he began. "Make it quick - we've got a lot to do today."

The sergeant cleared his throat. "Sir, we are a delegation here to ask you to cease and desist from the activities you and the company clerk were engaged in yesterday."

The Captain Was Angry

Suddenly, the captain was angry. "You, an enlisted man, are telling me, an officer, to cease and desist about anything?" The captain reached for his field phone, but the sergeant was quicker, pulling it over to his side of the table.

"Sir, we aren't telling, we're just asking. But if you can't, or won't, comply, then this matter is going straight to General Hays."

The commanding general's name was enough to make the captain pause. "If you're talking about killing those fuckin' Krauts," he began, but before he could continue, the sergeant leaned over the table, his voice carrying a steely edge in the quiet room. "That's exactly what we're talking about, sir," he said. "We know it can be considered legal. But the men of this company also know that what you're doing is murder, and we're not going along with it!"

Like air from a punctured balloon, the bluster leaked out of the little officer.

"So what do you propose to do about it?" he queried in a subdued voice.

"Depends on you, sir," the sergeant said. "You and your fat clerk stop what you're doing and never try it again - we'll back off. You try it again, and I won't promise one of your men won't take this matter in his own hands."

Finally realizing the danger his stupidity had gotten him into, the captain mumbled an OK, stood up, and put out his hand. Ignoring it, the sergeant shoved the field phone back across the table. "Call your clerk, sir, and tell him what we've decided."

Then he turned to us with a brusque "Let's go!" and led us out the door. In the hallway, he stopped, leaned against the wall, took off his helmet, and wiped his forehead with the back of his hand. "Thanks for backing me up," was all he said.

At supper that night, the sergeant sat by himself, and we didn't bother him. That same evening, the war returned with a bang. Our bridge-guarding squad had a brief but effective firefight in the dark with a German tank. The next day, the column I was part of, bound north for the Po, was bombed severely by what Fifth Army experts said was a German-piloted captured U.S. plane. I still believe it was one of our own U.S.-piloted A20A attack bombers. Friendly fire, on a major scale.

The war was on again for sure. None of us saw the captain or his clerk until after an early armistice was declared on the Italian front two weeks later. The captain's spy hunt was never, to the best of my knowledge, officially noted anywhere. But we had quietly witnessed how the deadly side of war is never just an attribute of the enemy. We had our own secret killers, waiting for their twisted chances to be heroes.

10th Mountain soldiers of a lead unit head for their next confrontation with the enemy in the Po Valley flatlands.

A LOAF OF BREAD AND A PURPLE HEART

It had been a day so full of unusual and dangerous incidents that one more just didn't seem possible. So I thought little of it when a medic standing in our first chow line in days said to me, "You'd better come down after chow and get that wound fixed."

"What wound?" I said, having forgotten my forehead was crusted with dried blood. When I remembered, and agreed to visit the aid station, it was just another reminder that nothing is crazier, or potentially deadlier, than a day in combat. This had been one of those days.

It actually started the night before, when we had fought a blind battle with a Tiger tank. Hearing the tank crawling in the river bed below a bridge we were guarding, we began firing rifles and BARs at it, knowing our bullets were doing no damage.

In angry response to our wasp-bite bullets, the tank

elevated its 88 millimeter gun and fired up at us, the shell pulverizing the bridge abutment, and shaking the whole structure beneath us. Then Sergeant Keyes got a bazooka out of a jeep, lay on the road's edge, and fired a couple of rounds into the dark where we could hear the tank's treads grinding over river stones. Both rounds exploded against something, and the grinding stopped. So we went back to directing the nearly constant flow in the dark of men and weapons that the following day would constitute the point of the Fifth Army's race across the Po Valley, and forgot about the tank.

Next morning, we were just a part of Task Force Duff, a long caterpillar of men and trucks and guns finally under way to the north. Not an hour into the march, a US-marked A20A attack bomber strafed the column with his 20 caliber guns, then turned and dumped a stick of 250 pound bombs directly on the trucks and men just 25 yards ahead of me.

Evil Looking Bombs

I remember lying on my back in a road ditch, watching the evil looking bombs exit the bomb bay doors and fall in a cluster towards us. Next I knew, I lay in the cornfield by the road, having been tossed over the roadside berm by the concussion. We lost a number of killed and wounded from that A20A's bomb run, which our statisticians claimed was the work of a German-captured aircraft. I still think it was flown by a confused U.S. pilot, but of course the Air Force would never admit to that kind of mistake by one of their fly boys.

The rest of the day was just as confusing and dangerous. Probing a side road for the enemy, Les and I ran smack into a German road block. Ditching the jeep, we had a brisk fire fight with the German gunners until they decided to pull out, but not before we both froze flat on the ground while a German grenade rolled down the farmhouse tile roof above us and exploded, harmlessly as luck would have it, right between us.

135

Later that day we pulled into San Benedetto Po, and instantly took shelter under our vehicles when a veritable rain of bricks, tile fragments and shrapnel littered the city's broad plaza, the result of a German barrage from across the river, shattering many of the city's ancient roofs and chimneys. Then came the order to guard the river's south bank. So I guess it wasn't surprising that I had completely forgotten the incident that had created my forehead wound, when the medic offered to patch it up.

It happened during one of the long waits, inevitable when a column is moving along a narrow road. Somewhere up ahead, the point unit had encountered German opposition. While they eliminated the danger, the rest of us had to sit and wait.

I was comfortably ensconced on the spare tire, manning one of our 50 caliber machine guns. The local Italians had been showering us with gifts. We already had a dozen eggs, several bottles of wine and a thousand Italian thank-you's. "Mille Gracie!, Molto Gracie!" came from every side. Then a farm lady, not to be left out, came running with her gift.

Simultaneously, the order came for us to pull out. As the jeep lurched forward, I just glimpsed a dark object in the air when something slammed into my forehead, and dropped into the bed of the jeep. Momentarily stunned, I slumped down onto the jeep's frame, until a copious stream of blood filled my eyes. Stemming the blood flow with my filthy handkerchief, I stared in disbelief at the projectile on the floor. It was a loaf of Italian bread!

Don't confuse an Italian oven-baked loaf with one of our soft store-bought loaves. The inside of this bread is soft and delicious, but the crust, baked in an outdoor oven, and inserted and retrieved on a flat wooden shovel, is hard as a rock. It was such a projectile, thrown by a well-meaning farm lady, which had cut my forehead wide open!

It's Good For Points

Miles and hours and momentous events later, I stopped at the aid station, where the medic cleaned and bandaged my "wound." When he was finished, he matter-of-factly handed me a form. "Fill this out," he said. "It's good for points, if nothing else!"

I read the bold print atop the form. Purple Heart, it said. I handed it back to him. "I can't fill this out," I said. "You know how I got this wound?"

So I told him, and he laughed, but then he got serious. "If you knew how many Purple Hearts are awarded for wounds stupider than yours, you'd fill it out in a heartbeat!"

But there had been too many of my friends who had earned their Purple Hearts with true combat wounds, so I gave him back the form. That night we hard-boiled the eggs in our helmet cooking pots, and stowed eggs, bread and wine in our packs. Crossing the Po in assault boats next day, and many dangerous miles by jeep and on foot to the north, we were grateful for that simple Italian food. Hot Army meals didn't catch up with us until the war was over.

Postscript: Weeks later, we learned through Fifth Army statisticians that Keyes' night time bazooka rounds had disabled the Tiger's caterpillar treads, effectively putting it out of action. We never knew what happened to its crew.

The sky was so full of shrapnel no good photos exist of this moment, launching assault boats to cross the Po River.

THE SHOEMAKER AND THE
OLYMPIC SWIMMER

It was the 22nd of April, 1945, and the 10th Mountain Division had just reached the south bank of the Po, northern Italy's largest river. While General Hays and the Engineers figured out a way to cross the river (the Germans and our bombers had demolished every bridge), we of the Recon platoon were assigned to defend one sector of the riverbank and keep our eyes peeled for enemy units.

We had built hasty emplacements for our machine guns, and were sprawled behind the lip of the southernmost of the huge dikes which bordered the river on both sides, alert for anything. Suddenly a machine gun began to hammer upstream, and we could see a staccato of pinpoint splashes stitching the glistening water surface.

Henderson, with field glasses, grunted "There's Krauts in the water!" Then - "Somebody's shootin' at 'em!"

Our platoon sergeant dropped down beside Henderson. "Gimme the glasses!" he ordered. A minute later he jumped up, handed back the glasses, and slid down the back of the dike towards one of our jeeps. "Allen, come with me, we gotta stop that!"

The rest of us heard the jeep roar west in the shelter of the dike as we gazed fascinated at the drama on the river. There had been six swimmers in the water - now there were only four, desperately swimming across the sluggish current, trying to escape to Austria under a hail of American bullets.

Two Were In Trouble

Then as we watched, the shooting stopped. The two leading swimmers pulled themselves up on the muddy shore and disappeared over the northern dike. But the other two were in trouble.

Still manning our one pair of field glasses, Henderson gave us a running commentary. "The little guy with long hair ain't gonna make it... he's sinking... the big blond guy grabs him... he's swimming with him!"

Meanwhile, the river had swept the two Germans almost in front of us, and Henderson ceased his play-by-play. With powerful strokes of his right arm, the blond soldier towed his limp buddy gradually to the shore opposite us, then dragged him unceremoniously up the slick bank and over the top of the dike. The drama was over.

"It was one of our line companies - I stopped 'em." The sergeant's quiet voice behind us confirmed what we had guessed - it was some of our guys who had been taking pot shots at the Germans. "They took a beating back in the mountains. Can't blame 'em for being pissed off at the Krauts. But shooting at helpless guys in the river ain't according to Hoyle in my book!"

Just then the lieutenant's jeep pulled up below the dike. "Change of orders!" he hollered. "Tomorrow we cross, tonight we get ready!"

So we dismounted the guns and trudged down off the dike. We were all a little shaken by the incident on the river. But the war wouldn't wait, and tomorrow, we too had to cross that deceptively powerful barrier, in fragile plywood assault boats.

* * * * * * *

Now it was autumn in Bavaria, in 1952. I was in Munich on an admittedly selfish errand, to buy myself a pair of expensive custom ski boots. A civilian with the U.S. Army in Austria, I found I could ski on weekends, so I needed a new pair of ski boots. In those days, there were only two great boot makers in that part of Europe; Haderer in Salzburg, and Hans Rogg in Munich. I had chosen Rogg because my occupation dollars bought so much more in Germany than in Austria.

In my battered, second-hand Volkswagen, I had been picking my way through the brick and concrete ruins of Munich, looking for Rogg's shop. Finally, over the below-ground-level doorway of a half-ruined building, I saw a small sign: "Hans Rogg, Schuhe".

Parking the VW, I stumbled over the rubble to the door, which surprisingly was open. "Herr Rogg," I queried, and a husky voice answered, "Ja, komm here-in." Inside, one weak light bulb revealed a counter, shelves crowded with new and old shoes and boots, benches, scraps of leather, and a small, dark-haired man in a leather apron.

Not Wery Gut

"Was wollen zie, bitte?" he said, and when I asked if he spoke English, he replied, "Naturlich, aber not wery gut!"

When I told him why I was there, and that I was an American skier, he warmed up immediately. Sitting me down, he began measuring my feet, asking, partly in German, partly in English, piercing questions about my skiing ability and my requirements for boots. Finally satisfied, he told me to come back in a month, and he'd have my boots ready for me.

While we discussed price, he kept glancing curiously at me. "You are older than you look, nicht war?" he said.

I admitted I was thirty that year, and asked him why he asked.

"You were in the war, then," he smiled. "I thought you had the look of a soldier! Where did you serve?"

"In Italy, "I replied. "In the Apennines. I was in the American Gebirgstruppen, the 10th Mountain Division.

"Nein!" he muttered. "Unglaublich!" and sat down heavily on a bench. Worried, I bent over him. "Did I say something wrong?"

Then he smiled, stood up, and offered his work-roughened hand. "Nein, nein," he said. "I just can't believe it! We fought one another in Italy. And here I am, making fine boots for you, an American GI!"

After that, it was like old home week between us. He told me his unit in the German mountain troops, the battles he had fought, the final ones in the Apennines against my division. I asked him how it had gone for him at the end. Had he been a prisoner of war?

"Nein," he grinned. "I was lucky. At the Po, we were trapped, all the *brucken* - all the bridges had been destroyed. But some of us swam across, and got home over the Alps!"

Now it was my turn to sit down. "You swam the Po!" I muttered. He grinned again, and shrugged his shoulders. "Well, not exactly. You Americans were shooting at us. I would have drowned, if my comrade hadn't been an Olympic swimmer!"

You Were The Little Guy!

Scarcely believing what he had told me, I then described, from my point of view, that April day when I had watched his life-and-death drama on the river. "You were the little guy with the long hair!" I marveled. "And the big blond guy was an Olympic swimmer!"

So we laughed and reminisced, Rogg repeating over and over that our sergeant had saved his life. Then he brought out a small bottle of schnapps, pouring my share into the only, slightly dirty, glass in the shop. Lifting the bottle high, Rogg proposed a toast.

"To us survivors!" he chuckled, suddenly showing a surprising command of English.

"To us survivors!" I echoed. And Hans Rogg's schnapps, and the shared memory of that incredible experience, warmed me thoroughly on the long drive back to Austria.

—

A road corner and low wall like the one where we engaged the 88.
Looming above Lake Garda, the first of the Italian Alps.

The Race to the Alps

The race to the Alps after the Po crossing was short, strenuous and frequently like a sequence from a spy film. We witnessed a German plane landing on an airport we had just captured. We watched an Italian train full of German soldiers pull up to a country station, where the Germans surrendered without a shot being fired. My squad had just taken shelter from a rainstorm in an old barn when a German 105 shell crashed through the tile roof, landed at our feet - and failed to explode! Then, shortly after a celebratory stop in the wine producing town of Bardolino, the shooting war caught up with us again at Lake Garda.

TANKS DON'T MAKE HEROES

It was a week before the war would end, but we didn't know that. The line company men who had led the attack along the highway all day were stalled somewhere ahead. We in Recon made our way up the sprawled column of jeeps, trucks and tanks in two 50-caliber-mounted jeeps, with orders to radio back to the Colonel why the attack was halted.

We were on the corniche road winding above Lake Garda, the turquoise lake below, gray limestone cliffs above, under a cloudless Italian sky. Every jeep, truck and tank in the column, including ours, was festooned with April flowers; lilacs, tulips, hyacinth, apple blossoms, thrown over our vehicles by the just-liberated people of Bardolino. Tucked into odd corners under our feet were bottles of the local wine, also contributed by the happy Bardolinese.

We had just squeezed past a Sherman tank which almost blocked the narrow road when the flat crack of a German 88 and the almost simultaneous rattling smash of a shell hitting the cliff ahead told us we'd found the problem.

Bailing out of our jeeps in a hurry, we joined a line-company sergeant behind the low stone wall edging the road on the lake side. Between successive exploding shells the sergeant laid it out for us.

"My guys are pinned down around the bend, behind the wall. The Kraut gun's across the bay. No way we can move ahead without more firepower.

I looked back at the tank looming behind us. "What

the hell good is that tin can if he can't take out an 88?"

The sergeant spat, and grimaced at the tank. " Yeah, I talked to the commander, a lieutenant. He claims he can't move up and engage the Krauts without radio orders from his CO. I claim he's just chicken, waiting for the war to end."

While Les got on the radio to the Colonel, Smoky and I crawled around the corner and inched ourselves high enough to stare across the bay. There in an olive grove the German cannon with its half-track towing vehicle squatted in the shade, silent for a moment, but menacing.

A Sherman tank in action in Europe. This tank commander is leading his men from the turret, not waiting for orders.

"Whaddaya think?", Smoky asked. "Could we do any good with the 50s?" I swallowed hard. "With a lucky shot, maybe. But this wall doesn't cover shit if you're sitting in a jeep."

Smoky grinned. "Yeah, but we got a windshield for armor."

Les hollered then. "The Colonel's coming up - says he wants to talk to that tank commander. Meanwhile, this damn war's goin' nowhere."

Smoky and the sergeant had crawled back to us, and were gesturing at the Germans across the bay. Another shell crashed on the cliff, just feet above the GI's lying behind the wall. The sergeant returned around the corner on his belly to check on his men. Smoky turned back to us. He was our squad's ranking non-com, a buck sergeant.

"It's this friggin' simple," he grunted. "Somebody's gonna get killed if we wait for that tanker. I vote we try with the 50s. Can't do any more than get killed ourselves."

We looked furtively at one another. Les shrugged. Henderson looked at the tank, then at us, and he shrugged. I looked at Smoky.

There's a War On!

"OK, it's unanimous. Let's saddle up, there's a war on!" Smoky talked like that - he was a cowhand back home, and a horse cavalry private before he joined us.

We hustled, bent-over, back to our jeeps, though the German gunners couldn't see us this far behind the bend. We stripped the flowers off the guns and gun mounts, checked that rounds were in the chambers and bullet-belts folded smoothly. Les and I started the jeeps, with Smoky and Henderson on the guns. In spite of Smoky's joke, our windshields lay flat on the hood, as they had throughout the campaign.

Les and Smoky led off with cowboy yells, Henderson and I in echelon behind them. We rounded the cliff corner, and both jeeps nosed up against the wall. As we lurched to a stop, Smoky and Henderson began firing over our heads. I remember the 88's muzzle tracking towards us, the hammering of the 50s loud in my ears, and our tracer rounds striking sparks off the gun mount and the tracked vehicle behind. There was a flash of flame, a plume of black smoke, and suddenly the gun was shrouded in smoke and streaks of fire

Smoky hollered "Keep firing!" We saw the bent figures of the German gunners running away out of the
smoke, and then all along the wall the line company
riflemen and machine gunners added their bullets to the
hail of metal that shredded the olive grove. The 88, as it
turned out, never fired again. Apparently, our bullets
had ignited the Germans' fuel cans, burning both the
tracked vehicle and part of the gun.

Move Out

Our 50s fell silent, and one by one the line company
guns did too. Along the wall, men stood up and
stretched. We heard the sergeant holler "Move out " and
the long caterpillar of dogfaces slogged forward toward
their next encounter with the enemy.

We backed the jeeps out of the way, so the motorized
column could get started again. Soon the tank, which
had never fired a shot, clanked by with its turret but-
toned up, as if its commander were ashamed to be seen
by us foot soldiers. We later heard the Colonel had
chewed him out mercilessly, but too late for him to contribute to the fire fight. We also heard the 5th Army statisticians credited us with one destroyed 88 and its tractor. But while they were studying the burned-out gun,
we were back on foot chasing an SS patrol retreating up
the steep sides of Monte Baldo towards Austria.

One of the Lake Garda wood boats at Torbole after the armistice.
Note the plank deck which carried the five-inch gun.

FIVE-INCH GUNS AND SAILING BOATS

One of the least known but cleverest examples of a "field expedient" I ever saw in nearly four years in the army, was the case of the British guns and the Lake Garda wood boats. We were nearing the end of the war, but the Germans were desperately trying to keep us out of the Alps, the "Festung Europa" (Fortress Europe) Hitler had promised them.

We had had little resistance from the rag-tag remnants of Von Vietinghof's Southern Sector armies north of the Po river until we reached the foothills of the Alps. Here, however, SS, Panzer and Mountain Troop units had come together to put up stiff resistance. Destroying all the bridges and tunnels on the Adige river north of Verona, the Germans had left us the only other nearby north-trending highways into the Alps, those running southwest-northeast along Lake Garda.

As they reluctantly gave way before our offensive along the lake, they destroyed, blocked or booby-trapped every highway tunnel on the east bank, killing many of our men in the process. Our mountain-wise infantry had found a way, via the precipitous flanks of Monte Altissimo, around the tunnels. But the Division found itself in Torbole, near the lake's northern end, under direct fire from German Tiger tanks and other German guns, with no heavy ordnance with which to return that murderous fire.

Enter the British artillery. Ever since the April offensive began, the 178th Lowland Medium Artillery Regiment had been attached to our division. We had watched in admiration as these battle-hardened Limeys wheeled their big five-inch (technically 5.5 inch) howitzers, pulled by trucks, into action, giving us effective artillery support when our own tanks and tank destroyers were nowhere in sight.

Around The Tunnels

Now, the British colonel commanding the 178th, a

10th Mountain officers puzzling how to get around the tunnels through these cliffs.

weekend sailor back home in England, thought he had a solution. Why not, he proposed, sail his guns up to Torbole, around the blocked tunnels, in some of the local wood boats?

On the face of it, the idea seemed preposterous. The boats he was considering were probably at least 100 years old; broad beamed, all-wooden craft with lateen sails and no motors which hauled wood from the mountains at the north end of the lake to the stoves and fire places in the villages to the south.

As the colonel immediately recognized, the daily wind regime on the lake made this ancient commercial practice possible. Cold winds flowed off the mountains and down the lake at night. Warm daytime southwest winds funneled up the lake from about noon until sunset. The wood boats sailed empty before the wind and up the lake in the afternoon, on-loaded firewood brought out of the mountains on muleback, then sailed back with the wind to Sirmione or Garda at night. The colonel thought he could repeat this nature-assisted process with his guns.

Which, in spite of negative opinions from some of our land-lubber officers, is exactly what he did. I happened to be on the quay at Malcesine when the first of the British howitzers was being loaded on a wood boat. The inspired colonel and his men had created a deck from old planks laid from the craft's gunwale to gunwale, then rolled one of the massive five-inch guns on its big rubber tires, by hand, onto this makeshift deck.

Lashing the gun securely, the mixed crew of local sailors and artillerymen swung the ungainly lateen-sailed craft out into the brisk afternoon breeze and sailed out of sight up the lake At least two other wood boats sailed two more guns to Torbole, but my job kept me from observing the embarkations.

The next day, I sailed aboard a DUKW, a truck operable in water, to Torbole, and learned there the sequel to this unique maritime maneuver. From the Torbole quay, DUKW's and our willing U.S. infantrymen hauled the guns to a nearby orchard, where the Limey gunners immediately engaged the panzers, perched on the road to Nago, where the 86th was still fighting Germans. Two days later, as we drove north towards the Austrian border, I saw the shattered wrecks of two German tanks, eloquent evidence of the skill of the British gunners.

Postscript: If I'm not mistaken, the official history of the 10th credits the DUKWs for transporting the British guns. But DUKWs were not big enough to haul even one of the big five-inchers. And this kind of mistaken history fails totally to credit an imaginative tour-de-force by an inventive British colonel and his men.

Peacetime Adventures

World War II ended for us on May 2nd, six days before the definitive theater-wide VE Day on May 8th. After a sequence of melodramatic events involving capturing German stores of liquor, and arresting Nazi big wigs in mountain-top hotels in northern Italy, we were sent to the Yugoslav border along the Isonzo river. Our mission was keeping the Italians and Yugoslavs apart until a border commission settled where their boundaries should be. Then we had a few weeks to experience some "peacetime" adventures, before returning home.

THE MARMOLADA

Not long after the war ended, three of us decided, as part of the latest official "mountain recreation" policy, to try to climb up and ski down the Marmolada, an almost 11,000-foot glacier-clad mountain east of Bolzano.

That late in the year (it was already June), there were only three places in Italy where we could certainly find spring skiing; Mt. Mangart in the Julian Alps, the Marmolada in the central Dolomites, and the Reschen Pass near the Swiss border. Since we had units near Mangart and the Reschen Pass, and none near the Marmolada, we decided to get in some skiing there before our duties as mountain school instructors would begin.

How we acquired a GM half-ton truck is beyond me today, but one afternoon we set out on the narrow, twisting road to Canazei, one officer, two enlisted men, heavy packs, three pairs of skis, and no idea what lay in store for us. After several false starts, we found the even narrower road to the Marmolada rifugio, and pulled in to a tiny parking space just at sunset.

Above us to the south, the looming mass of Marmolada's north side glacier still reflected the rose-tinted sunset light. Close above us, the dark outlines of the rifugio suddenly were lit by a lamp held on the terrace by the proprietor, who called a welcome in Italian.

Lieutenant Barker, who was fluent in German, responded in that language. Soon, as we climbed the stone stairs to the terrace, Barker and the "hut meister" were sharing information while Dick Wright and I quickly found our rooms, stowed our gear, and went back down to bring up our skis. That region of the Dolomites, of course, had been part of Austria until 1919, so our rifugio major domo, whose name, appropriately enough, was Guido Strasser, was more at home in Tyrolian German than Italian!

When he learned we had brought a treasure in C-rations, plus butter, bacon, spam, powdered eggs and potatoes, and American cigarettes, Guido bustled us into his kitchen, and assigned jobs to each of us. In no time, we were sitting down to a relatively elaborate dinner, topped off with some Italian wine which Guido had found somewhere.

Exploring the Marmolada

In between drinks and cigarettes, Guido listened to our plans for exploring the Marmolada. Since we were the vanguard of the "mountain recreation" group from the 10th Mountain Division, we were the first Americans to penetrate his mountain hideaway.

"First," he began, with the lieutenant translating, "you must understand, we can't let you climb without a guide! There are too many dangers on this mountain - rotten snow, crevasses, rock fall! We can't let you go by yourselves!"

To the three of us, who considered ourselves pretty good mountaineers, Guido's caution seemed a little much. But the lieutenant nodded, and Guido continued. "There is a fine guide, coming up tomorrow. I'm sure he'll be happy to guide you." After a moment, as if entertaining a second thought, Guido lay his finger alongside his nose, a typical Italian gesture. "Of course, he will have to charge you something - not much, you understand. Will that be a problem?"

Barker assured him it would not, then we bid Guido good night and climbed the polished wooden stairs to our quarters. At his door, Barker grinned at us. "Might as well go along with a guide tomorrow. Then we should be able to manage by ourselves!"

After breakfast next morning, Guido assured us that our guide would arrive soon, so we occupied ourselves with waxing our skis, and checking other gear for the climb. We planned on spending the night on top, so part of the routine was airing out sleeping bags on the sunny rock ledges outside the rifugio.

By eleven o'clock, we had all but decided to start the climb without a guide when we heard voices on the trail, and watched a spry but somewhat ragged Italian mountaineer approach, at the head of a gaggle of rucksack-bearing GI's, the first of the men we were to instruct in mountain skills from the division. Always a thoughtful officer, Barker asked if any of the men were interested in a climb, but none wanted anything but rest - they had been forced to hike from the road head in the valley with full packs. Their skis and climbing gear would follow on trucks.

So we waited for the guide, whose name Guido told us was Tito Cassin, to finish a quick lunch. Joining us on the terrace, Tito made a fuss about inspecting our gear, then, shouldering his beat-up skis, poles and pack, led the way along the trail to the glacier.

The first quarter-mile skirted the ice, which lay, covered with dirty snow, rocks and gravel, to our right as we climbed. In his mixture of broken English, German and Italian, Tito repeated Guido's recital of the mountain's dangers, but so far we saw only the normal glacier-edge terrain, now traceried with tiny rivulets of melting snow. As he emphasized the dangers, we wondered why he had brought neither ice axe, nor rope, nor obvious supplies of pitons and carabiners. Evidently, he was counting on us Americans to supply what was needed.

The northside glaciers of the Marmolada. Our route led from lower left to the summit hut below the highest peak.

Avanti!

Almost without warning, the trail ended at the edge of an expanse of spring snow, which rolled upward above us as far as we could see. Tito immediately put down his skis and poles, pulled a pair of worn sealskins from his pack, fixed them to his skis, and set out climbing with a cheery "Avanti, avanti!"

Lieutenant Barker, an experienced mountaineer, kicked the hard-packed snow. "Anyone want to use skins? Looks easier just to climb on foot until the snow gets soft!

So we continued the climb, with skis over shoulders, setting a track straight up the slope, while Tito laboriously zig-zagged ahead of us. It began to be obvious that our guide was not as experienced, at least on snow, as we had been led to believe.

But such matters seemed of no importance as we gained altitude, and occasionally glanced over our shoulders. Revealed little by little as we climbed, the scenery to the north became progressively more breathtaking. Nearby was a series of serrated ridges, mantled with dark forest, with glimpses of green farmland below, dotted with wood-roofed farm buildings. Beyond loomed the red-gray cliffs of the Sella group above Pordoi Pass, where we knew some of our buddies were holding a climbing school.

It was our first real introduction to the spectacular scenery of the Dolomites. Barker called a halt so he could take some pictures, while Dick Wright and I sat on our skis, chewed on K-ration fruit bars, and soaked up the view. Tito joined us, lit an American cigarette, and seemed happy silently to enjoy the expanse of his homeland below us.

Half Ruined Structures

The lieutenant's abrupt "Let's move!" reminded us we had a mountain to climb. Tito resumed the lead, but this time was happy to carry his skis, and kick steps in the still firm snow. As we craned our necks upward for a sight of the summit rocks, a new phenomenon began to reveal itself along the cliffs to our left. As if purposely defying gravity, a line of half-ruined wooden structures hung high on the dark cliffs, shocking us with their contrast to the pristine rock and snow around us.

"Baracche Tedescho," Tito grunted. "German barracks, from the Great War!"

Barker called another halt, "What's that building at the end of the cliffs?" he asked.

"An Alpine Club Rifugio," Tito replied. "Empty

since this war stopped most alpinismo!"

As we renewed our climb, Tito found enough lung power to tell us a little about the fighting on the Marmolada in the first World War. "The Germans (it was the Austro-Hungarian army, but he preferred the almost pejorative "Tedeschi,") occupied this side of the mountain. We Italians, the south side, even tunneling into the limestone cliffs of the south face."

Killer Avalanches

"The Germans slept in those barracks on this side. But they dug tunnels in the glacier ice below us, and stored their food, ammunition and other supplies, safe from any Italian artillery shells. On the 12th and 13th of December, 1916, in spite of all the tunnels, avalanches on both sides of the mountain killed more than 300 men!"

So we slogged upward, silently imagining the horrors of this mountain war, so much more physically challenging than anything we had experienced in the Apennines. Then the snow almost imperceptibly began to change. First it was a crusty half powder, half corn, then a powdery crust, then suddenly, wind blown powder snow, into which our boots sank to our calves.

"Time for skins, finally," said Barker, so we delved into our packs for Army sealskins, strapped them to our skis, and were forced to zig-zag upwards as Tito had done at first. As we climbed, the wind freshened, and the sudden chill brought out parkas slipped over our sweaters, and mountain troop hats pulled down over our ears. Eyes strained upwards, we climbed silently, willing the summit rocks to appear. It was Tito who announced the appearance of the tiny summit refuge, tucked under the actual Punta di Rocca, or Point of Rocks, which denoted Marmolada's highest point. Tito later told us, with some satisfaction, that we had climbed 1200 meters, or nearly 4,000 feet from the glacier's base, in a little over five hours!

The refuge was not at all like the comfortable rifugio where we had spent the night. A spartan box of a building, obviously put together from the wood, glass and stone of the ruined German-Austrian barracks, the place barely provided shelter from the mountain-top winds. But Tito quickly built a fire in the wood stove, asked us to bring in more wood from the splintered old boards piled outside, and soon had boiling snow water for us to make K-ration coffee.

"There's still light enough for us to look around," said Barker. "Tito, can you show us where we can see down the south face?"

Patiently, Tito led us outside, and pointed to a break in the cliff wall above us." You can see all you want from there - I have no need - (Non ho besogno) - to look down there!"

So we scrambled up to the cliff's edge, and looked

The tiny refuge below the Punta di Rocca atop the Marmolada. To the right of the summit the south face falls over 800 meters to the pastures below.

with wonder down Marmolada's famous sunset-lit south face. More than 800 meters high, and four kilometers wide, this incredible precipice was one of the Dolomites' great climbing challenges.

What A Great Climb
    Always ready for an adventure, Dick Wright leaned far out over the vertiginous cliff and laughed out loud. "What a great climb this would be, " he enthused. "What about it, Lieutenant, "Think you could arrange a climb for us?"
    Barker grinned, and punched Dick on the shoulder. "Let's get this adventure behind us before we start thinking about another! Besides, I don't know about you guys, but I'm ready for some supper and some sack time."
    Supper, reheated C-ration beans and beef stew, with a pleasant surprise, some decent red wine from Tito's pack, was lit by an oil lamp provided by the rifugio. In spite of board beds without pillows or mattresses, all of us were asleep soon after the lamp was extinguished.
    The air in the refugio must have registered near zero when we crawled out of our sleeping bags and faced a new day. Quickly, after a K-ration breakfast washed down with more coffee, we stumbled outside, once again to be astounded by the beauty of the mountain panorama below us. Now we could look southwest, to the astonishing spires and battlements of the Brenta Dolomites. To the west, the true alpine peaks of the Rhaetian Alps in Switzerland. And to the north, range after range of Dolomite towers, with the peaks of Austria visible beyond.
    While Barker took photo after photo, Dick and I and Tito stood astonished at the spectacle. "If we never climb another mountain," Dick said, "This view will have been worth it!" Then we began preparations for the exciting ski run to come.
    With climbing skins stowed in our rucksacks, we roped up, Dick Wright leading, me second on his rope, then Barker and Tito last on the second rope. Barker gave us the drill. "There may be hard-to-see crevasses in the glacier, so Tito will call directions. "A destra" means

right, "a sinistra" means left, "Halto!" means "Stop Now!" Any questions?"

We had discussed the descent the night before, agreeing to stay in the center of the glacier until we ran out of powder, then swing to the right onto corn snow for the rest of the run. It began smoothly, with Dick carving big, looping stem christies, me following, with poles in one hand and a few coils of our rope in the other.

A Council Of War

But immediately, Barker had problems, because Tito, after one or two clumsy turns in the loose powder, had fallen on his third turn. Hollering "Halt", Barker helped Tito to his feet, and we held a council of war. A strong, steady skier, the lieutenant decided to reverse his rope, let Tito ski third behind me, with himself bringing up the rear.

"Wright," Barker laughed. 'It'll be up to you to avoid any crevasses, and Parker, you'll have to hold him if he falls in one!"

Fortunately for us, there were no open crevasses under that trackless powder snow, so Dick and I made figure eights for several hundred yards until running out of powder, Barker and a harried-looking Tito following at a more conservative pace.

On the corn snow at last, we unroped and stored the frosted nylon cord in our packs. On solid snow, Tito's technique improved immediately, so we let him lead. With some photos of the German barracks taken by Barker and a final backward look at our powder tracks, and at the sinister ruins hanging above us, we free-skied the rest of the way down to the rocks and water and moss at the glacier's edge. Here Tito tried a snappy final Christy and sat down ignominiously on some wet moss. This time, we laughed together, happy to have climbed and descended on skis that daunting and almost mythical mountain.

To our knowledge, no on else climbed and skied the

Marmolada that summer. Dick Wright and Tito stayed to ski instruct our "pupils" on the lower corn snow slopes, and in climbing techniques on the nearby cliffs. New orders arrived for Barker and myself, so we had to say goodby, as our BLIZZARD newspaper put it, to our "Mountain of the Week".

Dick never got to climb the mountain's south face. Barker was assigned to set up college classes back in Florence. And I had another adventure by jeep in Austria and Germany. But we all agreed, as Dick had said, that if we never climbed another mountain, the Marmolada was worth every hour we spent on its snow-and-ice mantled slopes.

Four younger soldiers soak up mountain wisdom from
Joe Frankenstein, left, in San Diego, 1943. His listeners
from left, Korban, Landry, the author and Risom.

AN UNLIKELY ENCOUNTER

In late May or early June, 1945, Lieutenants Russ
McJury and Len Landry, along with Sergeant Sigi Engl,
were setting out by jeep from 87th headquarters at
Caporetto on a quixotic pilgrimage to Austria and
Bavaria. They were going to search for American and
Austrian friends and family thought to be stationed, or
living, in those former enemy enclaves. To give matters
an official appearance, the two officers dragooned me
from my mountain climbing and skiing pursuits to serve
as putative "driver" for the expedition.

Our first stop was to be Innsbruck, Austria, where
Sigi remembered his uncle had lived before the war. As
we GI Argonauts wound down the last slopes of the
Brenner Pass, we could see the little-damaged Baroque
towers of old Innsbruck, but also noted an area east of
the city where Allied bombs had flattened everything.

Once in the city, Sigi guided us among the shattered ruins of Innsbruck's main rail station and rail yards. Engl, stunned by the wreckage, soon admitted that the apartments where his uncle and his family had lived had literally been wiped off the map. Saddened and chastened by this setback, we found our way to American military government headquarters, to seek information about Sigi's uncle. As we stopped in a parking lot composed of bulldozed concrete, stone and brick, a small European convertible pulled up beside us, and a lanky American officer unfolded himself from the driver's seat. Approaching the officer to ask directions, I suddenly stopped short and exclaimed, "Joe, for God's sake!"

Mysteriously, the officer vigorously shook his head, lay his finger across his lips, and said quietly, "At the moment, at least, I'm not Joe!" Then he handed me a calling card, and said, again quietly, "Here's where you'll find me. Give me a half-hour or so. And remember, I'm now Lieutenant Wolfe." Then he walked quickly into the headquarters building.

That Guy's Joe Frankenstein!
The three others gathered around me to demand what was going on. Infected by Lieutenant Wolfe's secrecy, I whispered, "That guy's Joe Frankenstein, formerly 87th Recon. Now, who knows what he's up to!" McJury, as CO of the little group, suggested we try to find Sigi's uncle before probing further into the Joe Frankenstein mystery. An hour later, we had established through the Displaced Person's office that the uncle was not on the current displaced persons rolls, and that we had best look for him at the family's main home in Kitzbuhel. Then the four of us found "Lt. Wolfe's" closet-sized office, and gathered inside. Warmly greeting me and Landry, whom he also knew, Wolfe then sat at his GI metal desk and in a voice barely above a whisper, briefly brought us up to date.

"I left you guys at Camp Hale to join the OSS (Office of Strategic Services). Of course I couldn't tell anybody - the outfit's supposedly secret, even within the military! They gave me all kinds of hush-hush training, and dropped me by parachute into the Austrian Alps. Now here I am, under an assumed name to protect my identity, responsible for culling the Nazis out of the hundreds of Austrian and German "volunteers" who want to work for the military government!"

We pressed Frankenstein/Wolfe for details, but he raised his hand for silence. "The walls have ears, as they say. Even my associates think I'm Lieutenant Wolfe. Why don't we have dinner this evening, and I'll tell you the whole story." Writing the name of a restaurant, which Engl knew well, on his calling card, the lieutenant ushered us out with "See you at seven?"

Sigi found us a small Austrian hotel, whose proprietor he had known as a teenager, where we could stay the night for a few cartons of American cigarettes. After cleaning up, we joined the hotelier for a schnapps in his stube. When our host left, the others demanded that Landry and I fill them in on the mysterious Frankenstein, before we sat down to dinner with him.

"He's an amazing guy," I began. "His real name is Josef von Frankenstein - he's a baron or count, or something. The name of the family castle, Frankenstein, or Frenchman's Rock, was borrowed by Mary Shelley as the name of the character who created the famous monster."

Austrian Ambassador

"Joe's father," Landry continued, "was Austrian ambassador to the Court of St. James. Joe was raised and went to school in England. When Hitler took over Austria, Joe's father, a confirmed anti-Nazi, lost his job. After a brief stint as an ambulance driver in France until its fall, Joe made his way to the U.S. A skier since boyhood vacations in the Alps, he naturally joined the ski troops when we declared war on Germany."

McJury stood up, looking at his watch. "Time to meet this fascinating guy for dinner. Sigi, show us the way, and quickly, if you're as hungry as I am!"

Engl led the group the few blocks to the restaurant, located close to the famous Goldenes Dachl, the gold-roofed balcony at the end of Innsbruck's Maria Theresa boulevard. Frankenstein was already there, and had a table tucked away from the other diners. It was clear that Joe, or Lt. Wolfe, still wanted privacy in which to tell his story. Dinner was simple; some kind of veal, dumplings and a plain dessert, washed down with Tyrolian wine. When the table was cleared, the waiter brought real American coffee, a small miracle in those days, and Joe began his story.

"As I mentioned earlier," he began, "one day I was at Camp Hale, the next on my way to Washington. Kay (his wife, novelist Kay Boyle) had to pack up our tiny apartment in Redcliff and follow two weeks later. By that time, I was deep into my training, the details of which are still secret, except that they obviously included jump (parachute) training. After several weeks, I met another ex-Austrian, a skier and mountaineer, who was to be dropped with me into the Austrian Alps. Our mission, in retrospect, seemed foolhardy, to put it kindly. We first had to find a safe headquarters on a mountain farm, then establish regular radio contact, first with England, later with U.S. operations in France."

Joe paused, laughing quietly. "That was the easy part. In late autumn of 1944, my partner and I flew as part of a bombing mission over Bavaria. Somewhere near Munich, our plane diverted long enough to drop us in the Voralps west of Innsbruck, terrain already covered with early snow, then doubled back to rejoin the returning bombers."

We Had Skis

Anticipating our obvious questions, Joe smiled. "Yes,

we had skis - Austrian skis, and yes, we used them. We found the anti-Nazi farm family which had been vetted in advance, and soon had radio contact with General Bradley's 12th Army Group in France. Our broadcasts were of course in code. Once we had established an observation post above the main north-south pass from Germany into Austria, our next job was to report in detail major military traffic in either direction. This was considered important at the time - remember, Hitler was promoting his plan for Festung Europa, Fortress Europe, a final refuge for the Third Reich, in the German, Austrian and Italian Alps." Frankenstein grinned at us. "My German sources told me that's why the 10th Mountain was inserted at the last minute in the Apennines, to deny the southern boundaries of Fortress Europe!"

Joe paused, stretched and ordered more (American) coffee. "Our next mission was much riskier; to capture a German officer, interrogate him, and radio the results to Bradley. And this is when I got the crazy idea that landed me in Innsbruck last February!"

Fortified with more coffee, and small glasses of schnapps (Austrians love schnapps), we four Americans huddled around Frankenstein, who hadn't raised his voice above a near-whisper all evening. By this time, the restaurant was nearly empty, yet the manager and waiter never showed they were anxious for our group to leave. Certainly, Lieutenant Wolfe had arranged for a really private evening.

"The next phase turned out to be amazingly easy. We had seen dozens of German jeeps (Volkswagens), traveling back and forth, sometimes without escort. I guess they never dreamed there were enemies in the hills! Our plan was to locate a small side road off a narrow place in the highway, and stage our ambush there. I was to spot our victims with field glasses, and signal Kurt (my partner) to drop a pre-cut tree across the road. It worked perfectly. The Volks stopped short, the driver got out to move the tree, and in minutes we had both officer and driver tied in the back seat, removed the tree, and had pulled the car up the side road and out of sight.

It Was War

Frankenstein sighed, and rubbed his eyes. "I wish I didn't have to tell you this, but as you all know, it was war, and we were in the heart of enemy country. We found a small hay barn nearby, and took the Germans there for questioning. Both were loyal Nazis, neither would, in spite of our threats, tell us anything. It was then I realized that the officer looked a lot like me, and the driver could have been Kurt's cousin. What if, I thought - what if?"

"Rummaging through the officer's dispatch case, I found what I wanted, the orders for his next station, and all of his personal papers. Innsbruck! At Kesselring's Army headquarters! The perfect place to report on preparations for Festung Europa! Telling Kurt the rough outlines of my plans in English, I ordered the two Germans to shed their uniforms and boots, and step outside. We walked them to a nearby ravine, both shivering from the cold, and the sure knowledge of their fates. With the officer's Luger, I shot him, and Kurt shot the driver with the same gun. When we rolled their bodies into the ravine, I felt certain no one would find them until spring had melted the mountain snows."

Frankenstein sighed again, and looked at us. "You've been there. You know how hard it is." McJury reached across the table, and squeezed Joe's arm. "We know. No need for apologies." Encouraged, the OSS veteran went on with his incredible tale of clandestine warfare.

"After dark that night, we returned by Volkswagen to our farm headquarters, creeping along deserted roads with just the machine's blackout lights. We garaged the jeep in the farmer's barn, telling the family nothing the captured jeep didn't already tell them. Then by candle-light in our room, we completed the details of my next impossible venture."

Noting our eager interest, he hurried on. "The next day we told the family we were going on a short reconnaissance, and headed for Innsbruck in the Volkswagen, each of us correctly attired in our doppelganger's uniform. I was amazed that there was only one guard station on the long road, which we passed with a brisk salute from the guards. In Innsbruck, I inquired our way in colloquial German, and by three that afternoon I was reporting to the officer of the day at Kesselring's army group headquarters as "Leutnant Hoffman" from the appropriate Munich office. Kurt abandoned the Volks in a military parking lot, stripping it of any papers, hitched a ride with a Munich-bound truck convoy, and was back at the farm the next day.

It Sounds Unbelievable

Frankenstein saw his audience was skeptical about this latest twist to his story. "I know it sounds unbelievable, but I was able to function for three months as Lieutenant Hoffman. With the special OSS radio I'd brought in my gear, perched in the top-floor window of my apartment building, I reported to Kurt once a week. But as you know, there was little positive news to report in those days, the once-proud German Wehrmacht was being beaten on every front. I heard of your major offensive on April 14 in the Apennines, then the very next day, my make-believe world collapsed around me."

Joe stood up, stretched, then hunched in his chair again. "There's little more to tell. I was seated at my desk when a colleague came in, his face all smiles. Hoffman, he said. You won't believe it! There's a buddy of yours here from Munich! Well of course the buddy knew I wasn't Hoffman, and in a matter of hours, I was stripped of my uniform, belt and pistol, and hustled into a cell garbed in some kind of gray cotton coveralls. Two weeks later, I was court-martialed, and sentenced to die by firing squad on May 10, 1945. As you know well,

General Von Vietinghoff, who had succeeded Kesselring, signed an armistice with your General Hays effective May 2nd, and a general armistice was signed on May 8th. A few days later, a captain from the American 42nd Division appeared outside my cell with my German jailer. At last, my secret, OSS-kind of war was over!"

We sat there, blown away by the implications of Joe's story. "Worked in German headquarters for three months! Scheduled to be executed on May 10th!" But we were to hear no more. Joe got up, smiled, and shook our hands. "Luck of the Frankensteins!" he said, and "Auf wiedersehen - keep in touch!" and walked into the night. None of us, I believe, ever saw him again.

A Postscript:

We subsequently found Sigi's uncle in Kitzbuhel. And I did keep track of Joe through military channels (I worked for the Army in Austria in the '50s), and through the news stories that both Frankensteins generated. Joe left Innsbruck when the French Army took over its occupation. Next I heard he was editor-in-chief of the newly revived Frankfurter Zeitung, which had been the New York Times of Germany. Under his guidance, the Zeitung regained its stature as Western Germany's top newspaper.

While Joe was rebuilding the Zeitung, Kay Boyle was writing perceptive but scathing stories about the lives of Americans in occupied Germany, some of which were published in the New Yorker magazine. When a German eventually took over his job, Joe and Kay retired to Connecticut, where she continued to write, and he lived the life of a country gentleman until his death. She, an incredible person in her own right, died a few years after her amazing, and enigmatic, husband.

MISTUH TRUMAN SAYS!

Our departure from Italy in August of '45 was as reminiscent of old Europe as our trip up to Livorno in the old sailboat-steamer in January. In the Florence railyard, we loaded into a string of ancient boxcars, pulled by an equally ancient steam engine. The cars were almost exact replicas of the famous French "40 and 8s" of World War I, and packed in them we rattled down to Naples approximately 40 men per car. It was stifling hot, so at night some of us climbed onto the roofs of our cars, and fastened to the roof slats with our belts for safety, we did our best to enjoy the somewhat cooler air of our "upper bunks".

The night air was heavy with the smells of Italy; flowers, wood fires, pasta cooking and the home-made soap aroma of wet laundry hanging out to dry. Tinny-sounding radios played seemingly all night long the familiar but haunting popular songs of the war years. It wasn't exactly first class, but we were headed home, so we didn't care.

In Naples, we filed aboard the massive troop ship Mount Vernon, which had been the peacetime luxury liner Washington, quite a contrast to our 40 and 8s! The European war was over, and though we had just learned the division was already chosen for the attack against Japan, many of us had high enough Army Services Record scores so we hoped we'd soon be discharged.

So it was with light hearts that most of us left the

mountains of war-torn Italy and steamed westward through the wine dark seas of the Mediterranean. Once past Gibraltar, military discipline relaxed sufficiently so that we sun bathed, played volleyball, ogled the few Army nurses on board and dreamed of the civilian lives we hoped to resume at home.

A Super Bomb
   In mid-ocean, news that some sort of super bomb had been dropped on Japan electrified the ship. What sort of bomb was it? Would the Japanese fight on? Did this mean no more war for the 10th Division? Then a second bomb was dropped, and rumors of war's end swept the Mount Vernon. Yet the big ship sailed on, with a sort of subdued celebratory feeling infecting every man aboard.

   However, our arrival in Newport News harbor on August 11th, the unloading into trucks, laden down with heavy barracks bags, and the short but crowded trip to Camp Patrick Henry, emphasized to all of us that we were still in the Army, and might be for a long time to come. The next day, men from every corner of the country streamed out of Patrick Henry, headed for a brief home leave. My group entrained for New Jersey's Fort Dix, an old camp where my father had trained dough-boys headed for France back in 1917.

   But it wasn't for long. With leave papers safe in the pockets of our Eisenhower jackets, and laden now with somehow lighter barracks bags filled with souvenirs, a happy gang of us climbed aboard a string of passenger cars soon to be attached to a New York Central express bound north and west. We were, at last, going home!

   Though it was a cloudy day, many of us sat glued to the smoke-grimed windows of the train, absorbed in the once familiar yet now exciting views of the fresh-painted homes, shiny automobiles, and busy farms and factories of an unscarred, peaceful America. As evening fell, we crossed a high steel bridge and began click-clacking up the historic east bank of the Hudson River.

With nothing but night outside our windows, we at last began to think of celebrating our return from war-ravaged Europe. Bottles of forbidden booze appeared out of barracks bags. Several, to our starved eyes, attractive young women, Army WACs and Navy WAVES, shared our seats and our bottles, and occasionally allowed us a stolen kiss or two.

One of our more enterprising buddies arrived breathless from forward in the train. "There's parties up in first class, in every compartment! C'mon! Everybody's welcome!"

So we jostled up the aisles, and looked into every suite until we found room to crowd in. I found myself with a noisy gang of guys and girls in uniform, presided over by an overweight businessman in a silk summer suit. Champagne, Scotch and gin flowed in and out of paper cups, as we and our businessman toasted the expected end of hostilities.

Anybody Got A Luger?

Sobering briefly, our host, parading his knowledge of things military, announced he was in the market for any kind of side-arm, German, Japanese or American. "Anybody got a Luger, or a Nambu 8 millimeter, I'll buy it for my collection!" he boasted.

I couldn't believe my good fortune! In my barracks bag, I had both a Luger and a P38, acquired from captured German officers in northern Italy. And I needed money, to buy a much-needed second hand car! Hurrying back to my seat, I dug out both guns, and rejoined the party. True to his word, our host examined the guns briefly, then, with a flourish, peeled two one-hundred dollar bills off the huge wad he pulled from his pocket.

"There you are, young man!" he crowed. "I get my guns, and you, I hope, get lots of good times with that money!"

So the train and the party rocked on into the night, while I sat in the corner in a daze, more than a little drunk, and very much amazed at my good fortune. In the midst of the songs and shouts and toasts that filled the room, there was an insistent knock at the door.

A Grinning Black Face

One of the WACs, as I remember, stumbled to the door, and opened it. The grinning black face of a Negro porter, framed with white, close-cropped hair and steel-rimmed glasses, looked in. "Hate to interrupt your party," he began, but our host waved him inside. "Have a drink," he said, "we're celebrating surviving the war!"

The porter shook his head "no thanks", and inspected the watch that hung from a gold chain on his vest. "Got to go on down the train. Got to tell evuhbody the news."

President Truman with a young army officer in 1945.

Something about the way he said "the news" quieted the raucous crowd.

"What news?" our host said. Suddenly, there wasn't a sound in that crowded space. The porter smiled, and seemed to stand taller, framed by the open door.

"Best news I evuh told" he said. "We jest heard it on the radio. Mistuh Truman says the wah is ovuh!" He smiled again, and bowed his way out through the door. It was the evening of August 14, 1945. And it was only then that our party, which had been going on for two or three hours, really got started!

Looking Back

Much of my experience in World War II doesn't appear in these stories. There were weeks, even months, of drudgery and boredom. Many conflicts with noncoms and officers, who somehow failed to agree with my points of view. The tragic toll of friends killed, wounded and forever mentally derailed by the traumas of war. And finally, the larger tragedy of nations against nations, shifting in less than a generation to new alignments, and new wars.

For many of my friends, their unrealized human potential was brutally cut short. For some of the rest of us, the war brought both bitter lessons and broad opportunities. Looking back, I know how lucky we were to be able to pursue the full and satisfying lives bequeathed to us by our less fortunate comrades.

With today's 10th Mountain (Light) soldiers belaying
from above, the 72 year old author climbs the
last cliff on Riva Ridge in '95.

The Reclimb of Riva Ridge

*The men of the 10th scattered across the nation after the
war. The stories of how they pioneered in the realms of skiing, mountaineering, sports, business and the environment
are told elsewhere. But this memoir wouldn't be complete
without a brief description of how a group of 70 and 80 year-
old mountain men relived the adventure, in 1995, of the
climbing of Riva Ridge in 1945. This article, which I wrote
shortly after our climb, seems the ideal way to complete these
stories.*

FIFTY YEARS LATER

On the wintry night of Feb. 18, 1945, the 1st Battalion of the 86th Regiment, 10th Mountain Division, climbed the forbidding, 2200-foot ice and snow covered face of Riva Ridge in Italy's northern Apennine Mountains, surprised its German defenders in their bunkers, captured several crucial German artillery observation posts, then fought off fierce counterattacks to take and hold this mountain bastion. This led to the 10th Mountain's subsequent decisive breakthrough of the Germans' desperately defended winter line.

Precisely fifty years later, though this time in daylight, seven veterans of the 10th, all over 70 years of age, ten hand-picked soldiers of today's 10th Mountain (Light) Infantry Division, two mountain and winter warfare instructors from the 172nd Mountain Infantry Battalion of the Vermont National Guard and a team of Italian Alpini veterans and mountain rescue personnel, reenacted the historic climb, considered by military experts to have been technically and physically the most difficult infantry assault ever accomplished by the U.S. Army under combat conditions. At the summit of Riva Ridge, the tired but triumphant veterans were greeted by five veterans of the the German mountain troops, their erstwhile adversaries in 1945.

"Riva Ridge Fifty", as the reenactment was called, was the brainchild of Santa Fe, NM, skier and mountain climber Bob Parker, 72, veteran of the 10th's 87th Regiment. Watching the 70 to 80 year old veterans of the 82nd Airborn reenact their famous invasion jump over Normandy in June, 1994, Parker thought, " If the 82nd can still jump, we 10th veterans can still climb!" With the enthusiastic support of 13 other 10th veterans and a team of young soldiers from the 10th Mountain (Light) of Fort Drum, NY, "Riva Ridge Fifty" became a reality just six short months after its inception. Managing the myriad details of the project along with Parker were Lt. Col. Larry Godfrey of the 10th (Light), and veterans Howard Koch, La Mirada, CA, Newcomb Eldredge, Newport, NH and Dick Wilson, Grantham, NH.

The original 10th Mountain veterans all agree they could never have made the climb without the 10th (Light) team. Freshly returned from police and humanitarian duties in Haiti, the Fort Drum soldiers, fired up by a chance for duty in the mountains, rapidly collected all the necessary gear; ropes, pitons, slings, carabiners, headlamps, harnesses, even MRE's, and were "mission ready" at JFK when the veterans joined them in New York for the Milan flight.

Support All The Way

Lt. Col. Larry Godfrey, the 10th (Light) team leader, and serendipitally also the 10th (Light)'s division surgeon, credits "support all the way to the top" for his unit's participation on the climb." Our division's mission is rapid deployment, and the ability to hunker down under difficult conditions and stay the course. Our division CO General David Meade saw the Riva climb not only as an excellent field exercise under tough conditions but also as a fine liaison mission with members of the International Federation of Mountain Soldiers (IFMS), specifically the Italian Alpini and the German Gebirgstruppen, and with the 10th veteran's organization, the 10th Mountain Division Association, of which we are members. So, with the blessings of our top brass, we were on our way!"

Traveling by vans from Milan to Lizzano in

Belvedere, 40 miles south of Bologna, the two teams settled into the Hotel Piccolo and immediately met with their Alpini counterparts to plan the climb. To their surprise and delight, the local Alpini veterans, under the inspired leadership of Sergio Tamarri, had not only pioneered a feasible route to the top of Mount Serrasiccia, but had built a narrow footbridge, a "passarella", over the swift and dangerous Torrente Dardagna, which had promised to be a major obstacle for the Riva climbers.

The veteran's "tech team", Parker, Eldredge and Bob Carlson of Denver, CO, spent the next two days with the Tenth (Light) and 172nd soldiers and the Alpini checking the route, installing fixed rope anchors and clearing brush where needed. To more realistically reflect the conditions of the 1945 climb, two "problem" areas were added to the easier route chosen by the Alpini. Under Parker's supervision, Sergeant Peter Gold of the 172nd led the installation of a 50 yard waterfall traverse, and climb team leader Major Gene Smith and climb leader Lt. Scott Ransom a fixed rope route up a 25 foot cliff. While this technical work was under way, others in the party spread out through the region, visiting historic landmarks of their 1945 combat experiences.

Violent Weather Ahead

On the night of February 17, which had been a brilliant sunny day, gloom temporarily descended on the assembled elements of "Riva Ridge Fifty." The Italian Meteorological Service, a notably accurate weather agency, was predicting violent weather; strong winds, rain and snow at Riva Ridge's altitude for the 18th, the day of the climb. Ironically, Sunday the 19th was to be a sunny, springlike day. The climb leaders were almost ready to postpone the climb when the always ebullient Alpino Sergio Tamarri pointed out that the meteo report for the 18th also suggested "possible" clearing and sunshine in the afternoon.

No Probleme
   "Andiamo (Let's Go)", Sergio said. "Climb in the morning, get wet. Sun in the afternoon, everybody dry out, no probleme!" With his characteristic cry of "no probleme," which became the expedition's motto, Sergio had convinced the other more cautious team leaders, and the decision was to go.
   Torrential rains were beating against the shutters of the Piccolo, and sluicing through the piazza outside when the team members gathered to load into the vans for transport to road's end at Casa Migliante. After careful daily medical checks by Col. Godfrey, when several blood pressure and orthopedic problems had surfaced, only seven veterans elected to climb; Carlson, Eldredge, Koch, and Parker, Dick Leo, Moretown, VT, Tiny McWade, Groton, MA, and Nelson Bennett, Yakima, WA. Also climbing with the veterans were Randolph "Ry" Ryan, a Boston Globe reporter, and Flint Whitlock of Denver, son of a 10th veteran and author of the definitive Tenth Mountain book, "Soldiers on Skis." Later shuttled up the back side of the mountain by authentic World War II trucks and jeeps to meet the climbers on top were the other members of the 10th veterans group; Bill Cruikshank, Neil Dearborn, Bill Murry, Carl Newton, Harold Paden, Fred Shuler and Dick Wilson.

A Foot of Ice Water
   Traversing the muddy trail from Casa Migliante, and hearing the roar of the Dardagna in the canyon below, the team was not surprised to learn that rain and melting snow had swollen the Dardagna so access to the passarella was under a foot of rushing ice water. Quick work by the Italian Mountain Rescue group in installing a fixed rope and brush and driftwood footbridge over giant boulders allowed the climbers to make their way gingerly across to the passarella, which was itself almost drowned under the torrent, and thence to the safety of the opposite bank.

The next two hours seemed unmitigated misery to the climbers, as they slipped and cursed and stumbled up the steep, rocky mountainside, lashed by a merciless wind, and soaked to the skin in spite of high tech rain gear of Goretex and Polypro. At the waterfall traverse, one veteran unclipped his carabiner from the fixed rope and, buffeted by the wind, would have fallen had he not been belayed by a young 10th (Light) soldier.

As the climbers wound upward, the driving rain moderated to wind blown showers and graupel snow, then a gusty but drier wind, and finally to blessed sunshine. Over the Dardagne gorge far below, a rainbow promised

Today's Riva Ridge in autumn from above Corona. From left, Mounts Mancinello, Riva, Serrasiccia, Cappel Buso and Pizzo di Campiano. Our route in '95 mounted the steep frontal ridge of Serrasiccia.

better times. The group paused at an astonishing cluster of ancient stone buildings that had sheltered three families of shepherds on this savage mountainside in the distant past. Here the route traversed slick slopes of grass and greasy shale and it was with a kind of ironic relief that they met the next major obstacle, the limestone cliff. Again clipped to a fixed rope and belayed from above, the veterans sensed a time warp, back to climbing training at Camp Hale, and to the blind, scary obstacles encountered on the night climb in '45.

Above the cliff the trail followed a ridgeline of Mount Serrasiccia, the highest summit of Riva Ridge, over more slick grass slopes, small steps and cliffs of shale and limestone, and brushy ledges. Here Sergio pointed out the layups of the wild goats, deer and sheep that inhabit this wilderness. Once on the ridgeline, both veterans and modern soldiers suddenly appreciated why Riva Ridge had been such an important objective. From this height, the Germans had enjoyed an unencumbered view of every hectare of the American occupied terrain below, and could direct pinpoint artillery fire on anything that moved.

Maddening Mud

Had it not been for the maddening greasy shale mud underfoot, the series of small faces, ledges and flatter stepped terrain on the way to the summit would have been a breeze. One veteran pointed out that instead of fretting about mud, the men of the 86th topping out on the ridge were for the first time exposed to potential direct machine gun fire. Fortunately, in 1945 it was night, and the German foe were asleep in their bunkers.

As it was, the seven veterans, two correspondents and their stalwart soldier and Alpini guides slogged upward in brilliant sunshine until suddenly there was no more mountain. As the German veterans offered welcoming handshakes, and the press jostled for photos, every member of "Riva Ridge Fifty" breathed a silent thanks that, this time, they had not had to climb this formidable barrier at night, over snow and ice, and under the German guns.

Col. Godfrey, a hardened veteran of Vietnam and Desert Storm, admitted that when he first stood at the base of Riva, it seemed a hundred times larger than the photos he had studied. "This son of a gun could kill you!" he had commented to a soldier standing with him. And German mountain troop General Gerhart Klamert, a veteran of the Caucasus campaign and Himalaya climber, had not seen Riva Ridge until the reenactment. Looking down the precipitous face of Mount Serrasiccia, he at first doubted any American unit could have made the climb at night, until his younger associates assured him the 86th had in fact done just that!

The mountain top ceremonies that day, and the elaborate celebration in the Lizzano piazza on Sunday were gratifying to the "Riva Ridge Fifty" veterans, but seemed hollow compared to the satisfactions of the climb. "Twice up that monster in fifty years," Dick Leo said to Howard Koch. "Can you believe it?" Koch grinned, "No, but we did it!" To a 10th Mountain man, that said it all.

ILLUSTRATION & PHOTO CREDITS

Cover Photo - Bob Parker

Page 2 - The author on skis - Unknown
    12 - Mount Rainier - Unknown
    15 - Summer on Rainier - Bob Parker
    19 - Mount Rainier - Dee Molenaar
    22 - Jolon Mission - Unknown
    25 - Tents at Jolon - Bob Parker
    32 - Soldiers, Homestake Peak - Bob Parker
    40 - Avalanche Ice - Winston Pote
    43 - Kiska Flags - Resource Center*
    45 - Map - Alaska & the Aleutians
    47 - Landing Craft Kiska - George Earle
    50 GI-Kiska Harbor - Unknown
    54 - Kiska Volcano - Unknown
    60 - Kiska Tent City - Resource Center
    73 - Kiska Harbor Art - George Earle
    79 - Ski Troopers March - Winston Pote
    82 - Camp Hale - Resource Center
    85 - Aspen, Roch Run - Miggs Durrance
    86 - Skiers, Aspen Mountain - Dick Wright
    89 - Recon on Bridge - Bob Parker
    93 - Mules, Camp Swift - Resource Center
    97 - Map - Northern Italy
   102 - San Marcello - Dick Rocker
   107 - Vidiciatico - Dick Rocker

110 - Corona - Dick Rocker
112 - Map - Sgt. Armand Cassini
117 - La Serra/Punchboard Hill - Dick Rocker
121 - Castel d'Aiano - Dick Rocker
125 - Towers of Florence - Postcard
127 - Stretcher Bearers - Resource Center
134 - Troops in Po Valley - Dick Rocker
138 - Crossing Po Sketch - Sgt. Bob Fels
143 - Garda Corner - Dick Rocker
145 - Sherman Tank - Signal Corps
148 - Garda Wood Boat - Resource Center
149 - Garda Cliffs - Dick Rocker
154 - The Marmolada - Postcard Dick Wright
157 - Summit Hut - Postcard Dick Wright
161 - Recon Group - Unknown
172 - Harry Truman - Unknown
174 - Riva Cliff - Ry Ryan
179 - Riva Ridge - Fred Schuler

* All credits marked "Resource Center" represent photo credits granted by the 10th Mountain Resource Center, Denver Public Library, Denver, Colorado.

GLOSSARY

Many of my friends and my publisher have complained that words are used here which many of my younger readers may not understand. Therefore, this glossary of words and organizations common to all of my generation, so that future generations may understand:

MILITARY ORGANIZATIONS:

The 10th Mountain Division after Camp Swift was organized as follows:

1. Division Headquarters, with a headquarters company, including a reconnaissance platoon.

2. Three Infantry Regiments: 85th, 86th, 87th, each with regimental headquarters, reconnaissance platoons, medical, supply and service units.

3. Each regiment had three battalions, of roughly 1,000 men each.

4, Each battalion had four companies of 200 men; three rifle and one heavy weapons (81mm. mortars and 50-caliber machine guns), plus a headquarters company.

5. Each rifle company (for example 2nd Battalion, Companies E,F and G), had four platoons, the last of which handled 30-caliber machine guns and 60 mm mortars.

6. Three squads, with approximately 12 men each, made up a platoon. Various clerks, medical and supply, cooks and other personnel brought the average company up to about 200 men.

7. Our commanding officers were: Regiment: Colonel, Battalion: Lieutenant Colonel or Major; Company: Captain, Platoon: 1st or 2nd Lieutenant.

8. Our non-commissioned officers were: Special Assignments: Warrant Officers, Company: 1st Sergeant or Sergeant Major, Platoon: Platoon Sergeant, Squad: Sergeant. Various special duties were handled by Corporals or T5's (Technical Corporals).

9. Combat deaths and injuries, illness and other emergencies frequently reduced whole battalions, companies, platoons and squads to mere shadows of their assigned numbers.

MILITARY TERMS
ASR - Army Service Record
CB's - Navy Construction Battalions
CO - Commanding Officer
C-ration - canned emergency rations
gunwale - boat or ship railing
KP - kitchen police
K-ration - packaged emergency rations
MRE's - meals ready to eat
on point - first man leading a patrol
op - observation post
OSS. -Office of Special Services (today's CIA)
pyramidal tent - squad tent with pyramidal top
remount - horses to replace or add to cavalry unit
Recon - Reconnaissance platoon
slit trench - narrow trench for latrine or defense
SNAFU - situation normal all fouled up
Wehrmacht - German Army

MILITARY VEHICLES AND WEAPONS:
BAR - large, heavy, fully-automatic machine rifle
bazooka - shoulder mounted U.S. rocket launcher
bouncing betty - deadly German mine
carbine - small, light 30-caliber Garand rifle
davits - frames to hold and lower lifeboats
DUKW - truck operable in water
88 - German 88-millimeter cannon
.45 - U.S. 45-caliber pistol
Garand - larger standard 30-caliber Garand rifle
Higgins Boat - landing craft with opening front ramp
howitzer - short, high-angle cannon
LCVP - small personnel landing craft
LST - landing ship - tank
Luger - German officer's pistol
105 German 105-mm cannon
Panzer - German Army tank unit
P-38 - German Army pistol
pack artillery - U.S. 75-mm cannons packed on mules
SS - elite German Army unit
Side-wheeler - ship with propelling wheels on both sides
six-by-six - six-wheel-drive truck
weasel - tracked over-snow vehicle

SKI AND MOUNTAIN TERMS
boat tow - boat-shaped sled-type cable ski tow
carabiner - steel snap-link for climbing
christy - ski turn with skis parallel
cirque - hollowed-out glacial bowl on mountainside
cornice - steep snow drift on mountain ridge
crevasse - deep crack in glacier ice
crud - skier's drink; a milkshake and a shot of liquor
graupel - fine, tapioca-like snow
moraine - gravel-and-rock ridge pushed up by glacier
piton - spike to drive into rock for climbing safety
sealskins - skins fixed to skis for climbing
sitzmark - fall on skis leaving mark of skier's buttocks
snowplow - ski turn with both skis stemmed
stem-christy - christy preceded by stemmed ski
talus - rocky slope at the foot of cliff
tarn - small mountain or arctic lake
telemark - ski turn with one ski leading and tilted

FOREIGN WORDS AND PHRASES
alpinismo - alpinism - mountain climbing
avanti - forward, onward, upward
Bering Sea - sea between Russia and Alaska
brucken - bridges
doppelganger - one's identical or similar twin
Festung Europa - Hitler's hoped-for alpine fortress
gebirgstruppen - German mountain troops
40 and 8's - freight car, holding 40 men or 8 horses
Krupp express - incoming German shells
lateen - triangular sail common to Mediterranean region
nicht war - isn't that true.
rifugio - mountain refuge/cabin
torrente - torrent or river
unglaublich - unbelievable
williwaw - Native name for violent arctic wind